Energy

and

EV

Secrets

Dear Senator Pavley

How the Volt, plug-in Hybrids
electric cars and e-bikes
can save energy and
cut your gas prices.

*With appreciation for your support
and all that you*

By Russell Sydney

do

Russell Sydney

Speakers Press
California

Note: Various vehicle model names and brands are used throughout this book such as the Volt, the LEAF and Tesla. All of the manufacturer names and models are trademarked by their respective companies and no affiliation or rights are implied for this book. They are used for consumer comparison purposes only.

The links included in this book were functional at the time of initial publication and are subject to change. They are intended as an aid to further learning and are not presented as comprehensive listings. The functionality of these links is not the responsibility of the publisher or the author.

Review Edition

Published by Speakers Press, California
A division of New Energy Answers Inc.
www.newenergyanswers.com

Cover Design by Tom Kelley, www.tomkelleystudio.com
Graphic Art by Joan Charles, www.joancharles.com
Editing by Robin Quinn, www.writingandediting.biz

ISBN No:
978-0-9670308-4-5 (Hardcover)
978-0-9670308-5-2 (Paperback)

Contents

This is dedicated to the youth of today and to future generations. The intention of this book is to help create a sustainable transportation future free from the many concerns tied to the burning fossil fuels.

Introduction

Energy and Our Future

Energy needs are creating serious problems. There is at least one good solution. This book will give you details about how you can deal with both - the problems and the EV solution.

If you are fed up with everything that goes with filling your tank at the gas pump, then this book is for you. The book will show you how to stop the money leaving your wallet, your community and our country. When energy is cheap and you have the income to pay for it, then life is good. You virtually get to do whatever you want and have any goody you like. As energy gets more expensive and your income drops, then things get more and more challenging. Energy has been getting increasingly expensive.

Are YOU increasing your income to keep up with the increased cost? OR would it be good to find ways to cut your fuel costs?

These questions are good reasons to learn more about energy and electric vehicles (EVs). However, there are secrets tied to all of this that are being kept by select groups of people. These secrets can show you how to control your cost of energy, particularly the price at the pump, with the EV solution.

The *Energy Secrets* are actually available from lots of sources but they are kept out of discussions for two reasons. One is that the information is normally provided by engineering and policy wonks, which means that people fall asleep long before they get the secrets. Fortunately, the author has spent a lifetime learning how to turn dull technical facts into readable and even enjoyable information (see "About the Author" at the back of this book). These *Energy Secrets* have been translated into words and graphics so this book will only be marginally helpful for people's insomnia.

The other reason people have not picked up on the *Energy Secrets* is that they have very little vested interest in getting the knowledge - *until recently*. The thing that has changed (and changed repeatedly) is the price of gas at the pump. That is making the issue of energy costs something people run up against on a regular basis. Every time you have a painful "price at the pump experience," it helps to know the *Energy Secrets* tied to that discomfort.

The *EV Secrets* revealed in this book are secret for different reasons. The big one is that this is pretty new information. It is hot off the press, if you will. Things have changed on some very substantial levels in just the last year, let alone the past three years.

There is a second major reason for EV information being secret. That has to do with less than 2,000 to 3,000 people having the experience to be able to figure out the secrets before 2011. The author is one of those people and he has learned from the best of the rest of them. Only another 50,000 people or so learned the secrets by the end of 2012. You get to join this emerging group by reading this book.

The Energy Bill

Consider all the types of energy you use. It will quickly become clear that a big part of your budget is spent on the energy in your traveling, in your food, in your lighting and in your heating or air conditioning. It also takes energy to make all the consumer goodies and to bring them to your doorstep.

The energy bills that each of us pays all add up to the energy bill that the country has to pay. Throw in the energy bills that the government and business pay and pretty soon there is a really big number involved. Just as a really big energy bill is a problem for each household, a really big energy bill can be a problem for a country.

The details of this national and even global problem show how important it is for any responsible person to do what they can to help with this. The good part about the EV solution is that is helps with the big picture while keeping your money working for you. The EV solution works by cutting your fuel cost by over 70% and keeping your money in your local economy.

Paying for energy that is produced in your own country is a different kind of problem than paying for energy from another part of the world. Local sources of energy provide jobs for you and your neighbor. They result in taxes being paid to cover running the government and paying for government services.

When the money you spend stays in your local area, then you stand a chance of getting back some of it. If you buy a dinner in a neighborhood restaurant, the money goes to the owners and people who work there. They pay taxes to keep your community going. They may give some of that back by using your business or services. Perhaps they will pay you rent for a property you own.

When your money is spent to buy things made in another country, it is a lot harder to get any of it back.

Along these lines, when a big part of our country's really big energy bill goes to pay for energy from another country, that money has left the local economy. It is really hard to get the money back and it stops generating tax revenue. That means it is harder to create jobs in this country and harder to pay for running the government.

Is it possible that the cost of energy is impacting the economies of the United States and the European Union? The logic above leads to a clear set of symptoms and those symptoms apply to both of these economic blocks. A look at the specific conditions in the U.S. will put the global energy picture in better perspective.

All of this translates into a national and a global picture that gets really complicated. Here are just a few of the complicated questions that come up:

- *Does your country have the oil it needs for your lifetime?*
- *How will your national economy pay for the oil it buys from the countries that have it to spare?*
- *How will planet Earth produce and distribute the remaining resources peacefully and in a just manner?*
- *How will planet Earth handle the consequences of using all of the fossil fuel people want to use?*
- *What will be the impact of oil supplies on the quality of life and on the world political situation?*

In addition to this big picture or perhaps as a result of all this, the price of energy is constantly going up. The price at the pump has gone up more rapidly in recent years. The personal question becomes - *Will you be able to pay for the energy YOU need in the years ahead?*

Energy and EV Secrets does not intend to solve all these problems. It will focus on one part of your energy needs - *your need for transportation.* Transportation is one of the biggest uses for energy. Transportation has meant using oil for the last hundred years.

Gas Prices at the Pump

Let's face it; we have been experiencing an emotional roller coaster about the money being spent at the gas pump. It wasn't too long ago when $4.00 per gallon was a scary number. Then people got used to it. Now, $5.00 per gallon of gas is creeping up on the pump. *How soon before people get used to that?* When will $6.00 be the next scary number and who knows where it will end?

The gas price swings at the pump are more than annoying. They create a sense of uncertainty and anxiety. That is particularly true for people with fixed incomes or, worse yet, with shrinking incomes, as is the case for an increasing number of people. As gas prices go up, your money gets tighter, and some people have to use savings to keep going. Even worse, some people are getting deeper in debt while shelling out more and more for gasoline and other energy costs.

This situation can be described as having a lack of security about the energy available to you personally. That is more simply stated as a weakened sense of *personal energy security.*

It is possible to have a much stronger sense of personal energy security, and *Energy and EV Secrets* will explore that in detail. The bottom line, there are ways to stop being held hostage to the gas price at the pump.

The Secret to the EV Solution

There is a growing awareness of the need for better miles per gallon in our vehicles. That is leading to all sorts of improvements. Behind that thought is an all-encompassing idea that has been kept under wraps until recently. Just for the fun of it, let's call that a *not so secret* idea.

Energy (Not So) Secret
Energy EFFICIENCY is the key to providing for our future transportation needs.

This *"Not So Secret"* will bring us to focus on one really big change that can make a real difference. This change has just recently resulted in an economically viable and readily available solution. It will enable millions of people to become more energy efficient *right now*. That solution is to use **electric drive systems,** instead of burning gasoline or diesel.

Electric vehicles (EVs) may not be for everyone. They will not solve the whole transportation problem. They are, however, a really great step that you can take right away.

The information in *Energy and EV Secrets* will show you how it is possible for over half of the passenger vehicles to be some sort of plug-in electric vehicle. This is with the current models at today's prices. This picture exists now, and it does not require even one more public charging station to be put into place.

This is one of the best kept secrets about EVs. The vast majority of people are still talking about why EVs need this or need that before we can all start using them. People who know this secret are just driving EVs and saving a ton of cash on fuel.

EV Secret
*EVs could effectively replace over half of the passenger vehicles
on the road without changing the existing technology.*

Many of the people interested in EVs are just not sure if the vehicles will fit into their lifestyle. They do not know if they can afford them, or if an EV will give them what they need. They want to know when it will be right for them to choose an Electric Vehicle and which kind would be best.

Once you have a good idea about an EV that might be right for you, there are still questions that need to be handled. These questions have more of a nuts and bolts nature. They include things about charging the vehicle and how you would actually get around town.

This book as well as *Energy and EV Savings* (the second book in this series) will help you with all of that. Chapter 8, Costs and EV Savings in this book, shows how the life time cost for an EV can be lower than a comparable gasoline vehicle – starting right now!

Electric Vehicles have become a political hot potato. This has to do with them being associated with various environmental issues and other politically loaded concerns. These concerns can be divisive and controversial. That is why this book focuses on the concerns that are most readily acceptable to almost all reasonable people. These include the national security and financial well-being of the countries involved and the personal financial well-being of you, the readers.

A Look at the Facts
One unfortunate result of energy politics is it has helped create a lot of myths and misconceptions. These are being created by

people who do not seem to have the same facts found in this book, *Energy and EV Secrets*. The data in this book comes from the most reliable scientific sources readily available.

EVs help with an amazing range of current concerns and there has been a tendency to focus on how the vehicles help with these solutions. The many ways EVs help make things better is talked about EVs being *"medicine."* *Energy and EV Secrets* covers the medicine for the economy, for national and personal energy security, and for creating jobs. This book will bring in a large number of facts about these concerns. You'll get these facts so you can decide what is real and what is made up.

There is a lot more to EVs than the problems that they solve. They are great cars to drive and put "feel good smiles" on the owners' faces regularly. These smiles will pop up throughout the book.

Energy and EV Secrets looks at using all the EVs, from e-bikes up to conversions. Most books cover just the full-speed EVs, like the *Tesla*, the *LEAF* and the *Volt*. Some books focus on converting vehicles from gas to electric. This book's comprehensive coverage of the full range of EVs will let you find the starting point that fits your needs and budget.

Sneak Peak of the Price at the Pump

Here is a secret about energy and EVs to whet your appetite. Try staring at the following table for a minute or two and see if you can get the secret. The table compares the average U.S. passenger car that gets 25 MPG with an average All Electric Vehicles (AEV) that gets 100 MPGe (the "e" stands for equivalent). Here is recent fuel cost for the month of April 2013 for these two types of vehicles.

	Gasoline at 25 mpg	AEV 100 mpge	Savings Percent
France	7.69	1.58	80%
Germany	7.96	2.97	63%
Greece	8.55	1.46	83%
Ireland	6.02	2.19	64%
Italy	8.61	2.35	73%
Japan	5.99	2.20	63%
New Zealand	7.19	1.79	75%
Norway	8.40	1.44	83%
Spain	7.05	2.49	65%
U.K.	7.91	1.73	78%
U.S.A.	3.57	0.99	72%

PRICE AT THE PUMP TO GO 25 MILES
Gas Price vs. All Electric Vehicles (AEV)
in U.S. Dollars Using Average National Prices, April 2013

What are these numbers showing? They make it clear that a vehicle will drive 25 miles for a lot less money spent on fuel if it runs on electricity rather than on gasoline. This is what would happen with a typical EV like a *Spark, LEAF* or a *Focus*.

The data behind these numbers comes from the *Energy and EVs Book Two*. The most specific data is in the chapter called *Can You Cut Costs?*

This dramatic comparison may not fit your situation. However, even if you spent half as much on gasoline to drive 25 miles, you would still be paying more than for driving an EV in all the countries listed.

The retail gasoline price is different just about anywhere you go in the world. That makes it challenging to compare things from one pla∴ to another. This table can help with that. You can see that most countries pay one and a half to over two times the U.S. gasoline prices. The international price differences are almost entirely due to different taxes on the gasoline.

The spring 2013 price used above for the U.S. is lower than the price paid in California. This book quotes $4.00 per gallon frequently as that is close to the average paid in California for 2012. The difference is that the average U.S. pricing is about 10% lower than the California price and that is typical. That difference has a lot to do with the quality of the gasoline and a little to do with taxes.

These numbers lead us to an Energy Secret.

Energy Secret
It costs 60 to 80% less to run an EV than it does
a gasoline-burning vehicle in most countries around the world.

There is one country on this table that really stands out. It is an oil exporting country that sells almost nine times as much oil as it consumes each year. It also has the highest per capita adoption rate of EVs. It might surprise you to know that this country is Norway.

Norway is making money hand over fist from oil and yet it is setting both policy and domestic prices to favor using EVs. Greece actually has similar favorable prices for EVs but hardly produces a drop of crude oil. Perhaps they will catch up to Norway in EV adoption.

At a Crossroads

We are at a crossroads when it comes to the energy we use for personal transportation. There is a huge amount of pressure to change what is going on. That pressure is coming in large part from the many issues tied to Energy. High on that list is dependence on imported oil and how that impacts the economies of various countries and their national security. It is this pressure that makes it worthwhile for people to look at changing the way they think about driving and cars.

Chapter 1

National Security

National security is a common concern with differing views about how to keep our country safe. There are many who believe energy is a key to all of it.

What does national security have to do with electric vehicles?

EVs are at one end of a story and national security is at the other end *of the same story*. The thing that ties the two ends together is a need for oil independence. This type of national security story could be about any country that relies on imported oil.

Here are some viewpoints from national security and military leaders in the U.S.

Oil Independence is a top national security priority.

That is an opinion from knowledgeable authorities that is increasingly being voiced in the U.S. One of the first voices for this came from the neoconservative James Woolsey, former Director of Central Intelligence and former Under Secretary of the Navy. He talked about it at Electric Vehicle events.

After that, a whole series of Generals chimed in to affirm pretty much this same view. One of them is Brent Scowcroft, a retired United States Air Force Lieutenant General. He was the United States National Security Advisor under U.S. Presidents Gerald Ford and George H. W. Bush. Gen. James Jones is also reported to be raising the profile of energy dependence as a national security threat. Here is what the website for American Energy Independence quotes him as saying in response to a question:

"Why is energy a national security issue?"

"Our entire economy depends on the expectation that energy will be plentiful, available and affordable. Nations like Venezuela and Iran can use oil and gas as political and economic weapons by manipulating the marketplace. Half of our trade deficit goes toward buying oil from abroad, and some of that money ends up in the hands of terrorists."

General James Jones is a retired United States Marine Corps Four Star General. He was the 32nd Commandant of the Marine Corps, Supreme Allied Commander, Europe (SACEUR), and Commander of the United States European Command (USEUCOM). General Jones was National Security Advisor to the President from January 2009 to October 2010.

Another report found on the website for Cal Cars had the following quote:

"Fred Smith, FedEx Founder and Chair, and General P.X. Kelly, former Marine Corps Commandant and Joint Chiefs of Staff member, said that energy security was so important that far greater government involvement and regulation was required."

The following is from the website of Operation Free. This quote by Lt. Gen. Castellaw, USMC (retired) is from an article reported to have originally been published in the *Tennessean* newspaper. The newspaper website no longer contains the original article, which is interesting in and of itself.

"America's national security and economic vitality are threatened by our dependence on fossil fuels. For the military, moving away from traditional energy sources is not about being 'green,' it is about preventing any operational impact due to cost and availability of fossil fuels and the strategic need to secure fuel sources in unstable regions where our economy sends $1 billion a day to pay for oil."

Lt. Gen. John Castellaw, USMC (ret.) served as Deputy Commandant for Marine Corps Aviation from 2005 to 2007. He is a member of the Consensus for American Security and President of the Crockett Policy Institute.

The following comes from the home page of Operation Free. It is a website run by veterans.

"America's billion-dollar-a-day dependence on oil from hostile nations directly funds our most dangerous enemies, putting guns and bullets into the hands of our enemies. The Department of Defense has also stated that climate change poses a threat as well, destabilizing weak and failed states - the breeding grounds and safe havens for terrorist organizations like al Qaeda and the Taliban. With new, clean sources of energy to power our economy and fuel our military, we will no longer be forced to pay and protect regimes that support terrorism.

"America's national security leaders, including the Pentagon, the State Department, the National Intelligence Council, and the Central Intelligence Agency, are planning for the threats to national security posed by climate change. We believe it is time for our political leaders to join them at the front."

There are many military and veteran groups that are actively engaged in raising awareness about concerns around our oil independence. You can get in touch with the Truman National Security Project and the Iraq Veterans against the War. The veterans on either staff can help you get more information.

The information in this book will help you to see how national and global security is tied to the issues that surround oil. That translates into what our present and future military will have to do to handle those security problems. It means that it has to do with our present and future generations putting life and limb on the line because we use oil. That translates into this being about our sons and daughters and their children.

If our men and women in uniform are important to you on any level, you have the opportunity to let them know. You can consider how important it is to you to drive a gas-guzzling vehicle. You can show our military that you have their backs by driving energy-efficient vehicles. EVs are at the top of that list.

When people like these generals and our men and women in uniform express their sincere concern and give well-informed opinions, it seems like time to stand tall and say:

"Yes Sir. I will do what I can to help, Sir."

For many of us, it is hard to accept that sort of direction without knowing what is behind the request and why it is so important. Let's dig in and get that resolved for all of you.

Economic Dependence and National Security

It might help to have a better idea about the changes that have caused the generals to push for making energy security a higher priority.

The change that is on the horizon is that the West - meaning Europe and the U.S.A. - will have to compete for questionable energy supplies amid increasing demand from the other more than six billion people on the planet. Recent reports indicate *a fifty percent increase* in global demand over the next twenty years. The biggest increases in demand will come from China with 1.5 billion people and India with 1 billion.

The interesting thing about this is that the gas-guzzling world has a point of view which justifies this disproportional share of use versus population size. An article in the May 14, 2013 issue of *Newsweek* captures that point of view from the perspective of U.S. Energy Adviser J. Robinson. In discussing the need for production to keep up with *"international demand,"* he writes: *"Countries with large resources have an obligation to the world economy to develop their oil."*

That translates into the United States and Europe taking a lion's share of the world's oil. That is what it takes to maintain the highest consumption rates of energy and goods on the planet. This is done while the countries that own the oil need to use it to develop their own standards of living. That takes using the oil energy to build advanced economies and support expanding populations. Somehow the oil producers are obliged to give up their own future while keeping high consumption lifestyles in the western world going for the sake of the *"world economy." Could that be a disproportionate sense of entitlement?*

The impact that all this has on our national security can be clearly seen from looking at the list of countries with the highest proven oil reserves. This list has traditionally included the top three as Saudi Arabia, Iran and Iraq. Saudi Arabia was the home of Osama Bin Laden and seventeen of the nineteen people in the planes involved in the 9/11 attack. It is the source of the money behind that operation. It is home to the Wahhabi school of Islam, which has been repeatedly tied to the support and recruitment for radical Islamist groups.

Iran is one of the main focuses of our concern about nuclear proliferation. It is the main reason we keep a fleet in the Strait of Hormuz complete with one to three aircraft carriers. There are many additional security-related issues associated with Iran's support of certain neighborhood activities that include actions hostile to our allies.

Iraq is the site of the biggest war our country has fought recently that cost trillions of dollars.

All of this highlights a truly ugly part of our oil dependence and that is the part where the access to oil is tied into the worst wars on the planet in recent times. It has recently been made apparent that the situation in Darfur is being driven by oil availability, with China joining in on the financial end of that one. A similar situation is happening in Nigeria that also revolves around that country's oil reserves. Of all the Arab Spring countries, Libya has the highest oil reserves and that is the one where the West sent military support. The proven oil reserves in the Kurdistan area of northern Iraq increased dramatically in the first half of 2013. The oil can be piped out through Syria or through Turkey. Is it a coincidence that the violence in Syria has become an international priority since that realization?

The harsh reality for the United States is that we have built our economy and quality of life by using up our country's easily attainable energy supplies. The rest of the world wants to do that same thing with their energy resources. We can either figure out how to maintain our quality of life in some other way or be willing to take the world's energy to keep going the way we have. The rest of the world may not be too excited about that second choice. Clearly the U.S. Generals are not too eager for that to happen either.

So perhaps the generals do have a good point.

Can you become part of the solution? Reading the info on oil dependence that follows is one good step. You can find a way to deal with these problems and giving the EV Solution a chance may be part of how you decide to help. Then you can look every veteran of the war in Iraq in the eye and tell them you stopped doing the things that caused them to have to go over there. While you're at it, you might thank them for what they had to do.

Did I mention that former Central Intelligence Director James Woolsey really likes EVs?

Links on Energy Security

Operation Free
www.operationfree.net/our-mission/

Lt. Gen. John G. Castellaw
www.operationfree.net/2012/04/10/marine-corp-general-to-tenne
ssee-this-is-no-time-to-back-off-clean-energy/

Iraq Veterans against the War
www.ivaw.org

Truman Project
www.trumanproject.org

Misc.
www.americanenergyindependence.com/security.aspx
www.calcars.org/calcars-news/622.html
www.prnewswire.com/news-releases/repower-america-amplifies
-thousands-of-voices-for-action-on-clean-energy-and-climate-on
-historic-repower-wall-68659872.html
http://www.faqs.org/espionage/Ec-Ep/Environmental-Issues-Imp
act-on-Security.html

Chapter 2

King of the Road

Oil is King of the Road when it comes to transportation. The gasoline and diesel refined from crude oil dominates transportation fuel. The asphalt paving the roads is made from the goo that is left over after gas, diesel and chemicals for plastics and industry are extracted. The King fuels the vehicles and paves the way.

Oil has been the cheapest source of energy ever. It creates awesome fuel.

Energy Party

The benefits of cheap oil have been available to all people fortunate enough to be able to pay for it. Most of these people were in North America, Western Europe and various oil-exporting countries throughout the 20th century. The benefits started to move to an ever wider circle of people around the planet over the last twenty-plus years. It was a global party of sorts that depended on cheap energy to let the good times roll.

Two things have changed with the turn of the new century. One is that everyone wants to join the party and there are now 7 billion of us. When the cheap oil party started a hundred years ago, there were barely 1 billion people on the planet and less than twenty percent of them were invited to enjoy the fun.

The fun includes more than cheap fuel to cruise around the globe. It also includes all the goodies we make and transport into our lives by using the fuel - fun stuff like affordable food and clothing. Clean water is on the long list that goes all the way to including trinkets and toys.

Besides the increased number of energy consumers, another change is that the readily available energy sources have been tapped out - like the first keg of beer at a frat party. The rest of the energy sources are harder to access and are owned by an increasingly smaller percentage of the people. This is like a frat party with fewer kegs of more expensive beer and the party has grown by several quantum leaps.

Only this is not a frat party. It is a global economy with fewer barrels of oil available for each person who wants to use them. This translates into paying a higher price for the remaining goodies that oil helps provide.

Oil Costs

What will be the price of gasoline moving forward? That question is basic to *your* energy security as long as you drive a gasoline vehicle. The pricing issue is really big and complicated due to the global nature of the oil business.

That is one good thing about the electricity supply. By its nature, electricity is produced locally and for local consumption.

A Down-to-Earth Point of View about Oil

A recent conversation I had with an English businessman provided a very telling and pretty clear overview of the current supply and demand situation for oil. He has spent his life in the oil industry and made a substantial fortune. This was a casual conversation with the politically conservative semi-retired industry insider. We were talking about the state of the global oil supply.

While his point of view does not bring startling new info to the mix, even the well informed may get some value from what he said. He was clear about the situation being too complex to come to easy conclusions. The value of his view comes from how simply and clearly this oil executive made his case about some very complex things.

He was asked about the issue of how much oil we have left and what it would take to get it out of the ground. Even with thirty years as an executive in the industry, he knew that the questions that go along with this issue are so dynamic that it could go in lots of different directions. What he was also clear about is that the major discoveries of oil have already been made and that known oil resources are not likely to increase significantly.

His comments shifted to a different and much more straightforward level of concern. A level that was very clear and powerful. It is a poorly kept secret about oil. It is a secret only because people are ignoring how obvious this is.

Energy (Not So) Secret
We use the oil and they own it.

The "we" the Englishman is referring to in this "not-so Secret" is Europe and North America. The "we" is increasingly including the people of India, China and their neighbors. The "they" involved is OPEC with Saudi Arabia, Iraq and Iran at the top of the list. Canada and Venezuela have recently moved up to become major oil suppliers as well.

While we touched on this idea in the last chapter, the details behind this secret are worth investigating further. A simple overview of the global oil supply and consumption will give us a good idea of the challenges that lie ahead. The investigation will explore how these conditions will impact future costs. There are several big parts to the full oil picture with two big parts being the North American part as well as the global part.

Over the last thirty years, North America has consumed over thirty percent of the global oil supply. North America has less than five percent of the world's population. It has about six percent of the proven oil reserves. Production of U.S. crude oil has been dropping since the 1970s. The U.S. reserves have also been declining steadily up until very recently. U.S. production is scheduled to improve as discussed below.

Europe has consumed between twenty-five and thirty percent of the oil supply over that same thirty years. They have minimal proven oil reserves. Europe has twice as many people as North America, which means half the per capita use rates. Europe is reducing its use. The U.S. is increasing its use.

Asia (from India to China) has over thirty percent of the world's population and it has about four percent of the world's proven reserves of oil. They are just now getting to the point of using over twenty-five percent of the oil supply, which is up from around fifteen percent thirty years ago.

The Middle East had over sixty percent of the world's proven reserves up to a few years ago. Central and South America have just under ten percent between them as does Africa. Africa has one billion people out of the 7 billion on the planet.

We Use the Oil

The following graphics combine to tell a pretty strong story related to the statement from the British oil executive that "We use it and they own it."

The Oil Consumption per person graph makes a pretty clear statement in broad brush strokes along the lines of "We use it."

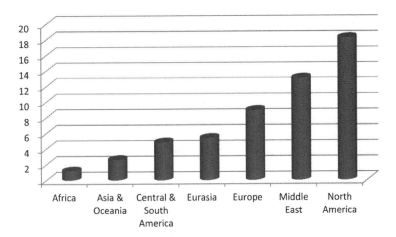

Oil Consumption per Person
in Barrels for 2011
Data Source: U.S. Energy Information Administration (E.I.A.) and
U.S. Census Bureau

Many people have some idea about North America being the global energy hog: still you may be surprised by the graph above. Even the countries from the former Soviet Union, designated as

Eurasia by the E.I.A., are using their share. The per capita consumption in the Middle East indicates a liberal domestic use rate. The total population there, however, is pretty low so the total oil actually consumed in the Middle East is not that high.

In addition, some part of the oil used in the Middle East is to produce the oil that is exported to other countries. *Perhaps the final consumers in the **importing countries** are actually responsible for using a large portion of the oil designated as consumed in the Middle East?*

The details behind the data presented in the graph above are derived from the data in the following graphs. The next graph shows *how the consumption adds up.*

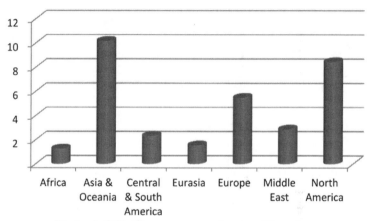

Total Oil Consumed per Region
in Billions of Barrels for 2011
Data Source: U.S. Energy Information Administration (E.I.A.)

While North America is using a huge amount we can see that Asia and Oceania (including India, China and their neighbors) are getting into the picture pretty well. It has only been in recent years that the total consumed by Asia and Oceania has exceeded the total for North America. Europe has made progress in cutting their consumption. The links at the end of this chapter will take you to the source of this data.

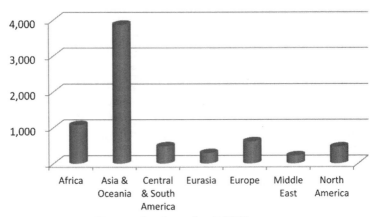

Population in Millions

Data Source: U.S. Census Bureau

The population differences above explain the contrasts between the last two charts.

So these graphics show the picture related to "We use the oil." Now let's look closer at *who* owns it.

They Own the Oil

Understanding who owns the oil and where it is located is an ever-changing issue. It requires getting clear about what an oil reserve really is. This is a little tricky because of how these numbers are reported and the politics behind reporting them. The most immediate needs for oil are supplied from what is tracked as the *Proven Oil Reserves*. A proven reserve contains oil that the industry accepts can be extracted effectively. Specifically, this is oil that can be brought out of the ground and processed in a refinery so that it is cost effective, as in profitable, to do that. An increase in the oil price allows more oil to be included in the proven reserves, as more money is available for the extraction. New technology that cuts the cost of extracting oil also allows more oil to be included in the proven reserves numbers.

There are politics behind the reported oil reserves. The most infamous one has to do with OPEC. The proven reserves held by each member of OPEC are a key element in determining how much oil each member can produce each year. The more reserves a member can prove, then the more oil they get to produce. The implications of that are staggering numbers of dollars. Another part of the politics has to do with government support, taxation and regulations of the industry. There are indications that politics is hard at work in the U.S. as some of the data below will call to mind.

There are several other categories to describe the total amount of oil in the ground. An *oil resource measurement* would be an estimate of the total amount of oil in place, most of which can't be recovered. The category of *unproven reserves* is the main one that has some sort of oil recovery problem. That involves the known oil not available due to some constraint, which may be cost or some other barrier to extraction. There is also a category for *contingent reserves,* which overlaps with unproven reserves. They have various barriers to use as well. When these barriers are removed, then these oil deposits get added to the proven reserve list.

There are lots of other categories for oil, including *probable reserves* and *possible reserves*. These are all known but have more problems with being available for use. More things would have to change before oil in these categories would get added to the proven reserves.

Then there is the oil that has yet to be discovered. These go by the term *prospective resources*. The oil industry has been looking for these for many years now. As mentioned, most oil people think that the big deposits have already been found. The consensus is that there is some hope of finding small ones which can be recovered at a reasonable cost.

It would seem that the exceptions may or may not prove the consensus about the big oil discoveries being in the past. A recent exploration effort in the newly recreated, semi-autonomous Kurdistan region in northern Iraq is proving to be huge compared to previous estimates. Here is what one article on The Oil and Gas Week website recently reported:

"Together, the Shaikan, Sheikh Adi, Akri-Bijeel, Ber Bahr blocks hold some 19 billion barrels of oil..."

That is almost as much as the total proven reserves reported in the U.S. as of 2011. This fact may explain part of the reasons for the many problems, efforts and tragedies that are tied to that part of Iraq. This turmoil is one reason these reserves were not previously put in the proven category.

It is possible that there are other parts of the world where exploration has been hindered in some such manner? Could there be more major finds that will impact the global market? This shows us why the English oil executive was hard pressed to come up with clear cut answers.

These different categories help you to understand why there are so many different ideas about the future of oil. To recap, this is a very dynamic market with proven reserves being used up and other reserves becoming proven reserves as the oil price goes up and as technology brings costs down.

The best starting point is to see how things stand. Then we can look into what changes are happening and how all of this might work out. Here is the big picture of what is known about the global reserves by region.

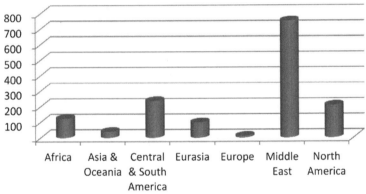

Proven Oil Reserves
in Billion Barrels as of 2011
Data Source: U.S. Energy Information Administration (E.I.A.)

Oops, North America only owns a reasonable percentage of the oil reserves. It is, however, a lot lower percentage than the percent consumed. Most of it is in tar sands in Canada. The discussion below about North America goes into some of the details associated with these proven reserves.

Interestingly, South America (at least Venezuela) is already dramatically better off than the numbers show. The graphs are using the proven reserves from 2011 data. There is more recent data released in April 2013 by the U.S. Energy Information Administration (E.I.A.). This data shows Venezuela has proven that their heavy oil and tar sands deposits, combined with the more conventional sources of oil, now hold over 298 billion barrels of oil. When that is added to the 13 billion barrels in Brazil alone, the total is well over twice the number used as recently as 2009. Note that the numbers used in the rest of this chapter are from the 2011 numbers, as that is the most recent year for data that includes the U.S. Proven Reserves.

One more graph will fill out the proven reserves picture. It is created by doing a little math that takes the reserves and divides the amount by the consumption rates. The result is on the graph Years of Proven Reserves. That shows how long each region would take to use up their reserves at the current levels of consumption.

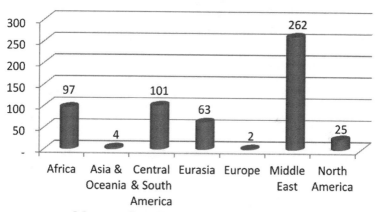

Years for Proven Reserves

This allows us to see that the most pressing global concern is how Asia, Oceania and Europe will get the oil they need. North America is next in line.

There are reports that estimate that the U.S. will match the proven reserves in Eurasia (more specifically Russia) in the near future. This is based on the more expensive unconventional oil. It would be a relief to see U.S. production improve as discussed in Chapter 3, *North American Oil*.

The European situation is particularly problematic. Only four countries in that region produce any substantial amount of oil. Norway, Denmark and the U.K. have reasonable amounts of oil while Italy has barely enough to make a difference. All the rest are virtually totally dependent on oil-exporting countries. Countries already overburdened with debt are going to have a tough time figuring out how to pay for their oil. Clearly, getting oil from the Middle East will be a big international concern for the foreseeable future.

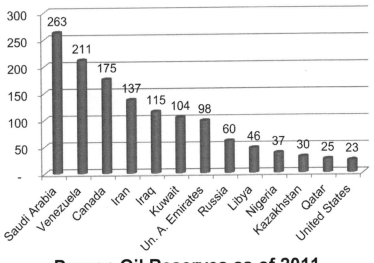

Proven Oil Reserves as of 2011
(Billions of Barrels)
Data Source: U.S. Energy Information Administration (E.I.A.)

The graph above focuses on the top baker's dozen of the oil producing countries. The United States was number 12 in 2009 with 20 billion barrels. Qatar has moved up since then, and it nudged the U.S. down one place - hence the baker's dozen.

Which of the countries on this list are you eager to send your gasoline dollars to?

It may come as a surprise for many people to see Venezuela and Canada so high on this list. Canada leaped forward in 2003 and Venezuela jumped up in just the last three years. This happened when both countries were able to include their tar sands deposits in the proven reserves.

The *World Energy Report 2012* identifies the main production growth as coming from North America and Iraq. North America is discussed below. Here is what the Report has to say about Iraq:

"Iraq makes the largest contribution by far to global oil supply growth. Iraq's ambition to expand output after decades of conflict and instability is not limited by the size of its resources or by the costs of producing them, but will require coordinated progress all along the energy supply chain, clarity on how Iraq plans to derive long-term value from its hydrocarbon wealth and successful consolidation of a domestic consensus on oil policy."

The report has a Fact Sheet that goes on to say:

"Iraq's energy sector holds the key to the country's future prosperity and can make a major contribution to the stability and security of global energy markets. Iraq is already the world's third largest oil exporter and has the resources and plans to increase rapidly its oil and natural gas production as it recovers from three decades punctuated by conflict and instability. Success in developing Iraq's hydrocarbon potential and effective management of the resulting revenues can fuel Iraq's social and economic development. Failure will hinder Iraq's recovery and put global energy markets on course for troubled waters."

This is a timely cautionary statement as the continued violence and unrest in Iraq has a strong focus on the oil industry with frequent attack on the infrastructure. That is reducing the development efforts as well as the total current production.

The graphs above drive home the message about who uses the oil and who owns it. That can be summarized even further by two more graphs.

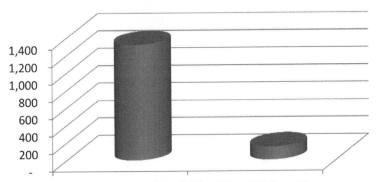

Top Countries Combined   The Other 200 Countries

Proven Oil Reserves
(Billions of Barrels as of 2011)
Data Source: U.S. Energy Information Administration (E.I.A.)

There are still large amounts of oil out there. However, almost all of it is more expensive to produce than past supplies.

Add the population figures to the picture we're getting and things become pretty clear.

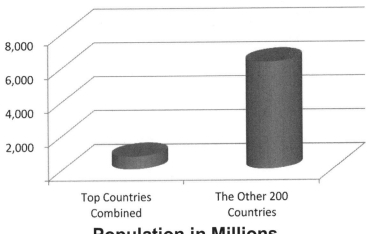

Top Countries   The Other 200
Combined   Countries

Population in Millions
Data Source: U.S. Census Bureau

These two charts show that ninety percent of the people in the world are going to need the oil that the other ten percent control.

At the very least, that will be a huge economic struggle. At the very worst, it will be an increasingly violent struggle.

It may be possible to avoid some part of this with new technology and new discoveries. There are some encouraging trends in technology that will delay the intensity of the struggle. That will buy time to find new ways to live beyond oil dependence.

The other trends are not as encouraging. These include:

- Oil production rates are increasing faster than new discoveries are being made.
- Major fields are decreasing in production all over the world.
- New discoveries are smaller and smaller.
- The rest of the world has been looking for oil pretty hard for at least thirty years.
- Large finds are still showing up but all of them are getting smaller and harder to find (with the one Kurdistan exception)

The struggle for oil means that oil will continue to be a volatile commodity. That volatility comes on top of long-term and steady trends toward higher prices. This combination makes it a poor choice for your personal energy security.

There is another solution to dealing with all the challenges outlined about oil. It is outside the oil box. It involves choosing to not be a part of this struggle. Electric Vehicles are a real choice that helps you to take that step.

Links on Oil as King

U.S. Energy Information Administration (E.I.A.)
Annual Energy Outlook 2013
www.eia.gov/forecasts/aeo/index.cfm
www.eia.gov/countries/

World Energy Outlook Report
www.worldenergyoutlook.org/publications/weo-2012/#d.en.26099

Post Carbon Institute Report, *Drill Baby Drill*
www.postcarbon.org/drill-baby-drill/

Association for the Study of Peak Oil & Gas
www.peakoil.net

National Transportation Research Center,
Oak Ridge National Laboratory
www.cta.ornl.gov/data/

U.S. Census Bureau
www.census.gov/population/international/data/idb/informationG
ateway.php

Wikipedia on Available Oil
www.en.wikipedia.org/wiki/Oil_reserves

Possible Crude Oil Glut Forecast for 2014
www.oilprice.com/Energy/Crude-Oil/Crude-Oil-Glut-Forecast-f
or-2014.html

Oil Price Forecast for 2013-2014: Falling Prices
www.forbes.com/sites/billconerly/2013/05/01/oil-price-forecast-
for-2013-2014-falling-prices /

Iraq's Potential as Oil Producer

www.oilprice.com/Energy/Crude-Oil/Crude-Oil-Glut-Forecast-for-2014.html

www.oilprice.com/Energy/Crude-Oil/Is-Iraq-Capable-of-Becoming-the-Largest-Oil-Producer-in-the-World.html

The Oil and Gas Week

www.theoilandgasweek.com/newdesign/index.php/component/k2/item/430-shaikan-field

PennEnergy

www.pennenergy.com/articles/pennenergy/2013/07/gulf-keystone-announces-spudding-of-shaikan-10-oil-field-development-well.html

Chapter 3

North American Oil

The history of oil in North America includes a trend toward more and more expensive products. Gasoline prices have increased an average of eight percent a year over the last twenty-plus years (see details in Chapter 6, *Personal Energy Security*). The good part is that there was plentiful and cheap oil for more than half of the 20th century.

The previously inexpensive sources of energy made it possible to feed unprecedented numbers of people. People have been able to enjoy traveling and an abundance of all sorts of goods and services at levels undreamed of by our ancestors. Inexpensive fuel has allowed cultural development to reach amazing levels and generally created a quality of life for many people at unprecedented heights.

The cheap oil times for the U.S. allowed it to become the most powerful economy on Earth. It rose to become a world leader, both economically and as the great example of democracy and freedom.

But what lies ahead for North America?

Oil Reserves

Proven U.S. domestic oil reserves are reported to have declined from the 70s up to around the early 90s when they leveled off, according to the U.S. Department of Energy (DOE). The Department stopped reporting these figures after 2009. That is the reason several graphs below use 2009 comparisons.

The U.S. Government is not currently reporting the proven reserves for the U.S. This is probably due to the impact of unconventional extraction technologies and how these are reducing the cost of producing oil. This combined with the volatile price for oil makes it difficult to pin down just how much of the oil resource in the U.S. can be extracted profitably. That will stabilize enough at some point to make new numbers possible.

The North American oil situation will most certainly include the tar sands in Canada. It should probably include consideration of the situation in Mexico as well. However, the state of affairs in Mexico is not as significant as the tar sands factor. The following graph shows why that is the case.

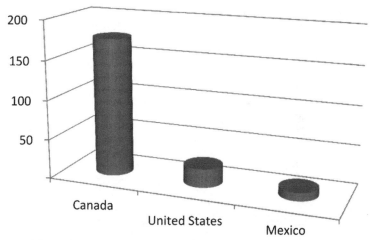

North American Proven Oil Reserves
(Billions of Barrels as of 2011)
Data Source: U.S. Energy Information Administration (E.I.A)

The previous chapter shows that North America as a whole has 25 years' worth of supply at the current rates of consumption. This graph shows where that supply is. It also shows where the dollars will flow to if the U.S. gets all its oil from Canada.

This graph representing the U.S. reserves may look very different for 2013. Unfortunately the Energy Information Administration (E.I.A) is still dragging its feet with the new totals for U.S. proven reserves. New data was released in April 2013 that did indicate an increase in this number from 19.2 billion barrels in 2009 to 23.3 billion barrels in 2011. The rest of the world has updated proven reserve totals through 2013 but the U.S. totals stop at 2011. That raises the question - *Why would the U.S. be the only country in the world without updated totals?*

There may be a need to take into account all of the changes that will result from the unconventional technologies discussed below. These changes have been known about for at least five years, so what is the problem? This may tie back to the discussion in the previous chapter about how politics plays a role in all this.

There is some chance that the new technology will only reduce the cost of production on already economically viable resources. If that is the case, then the net result will be an accelerated extraction and consumption on a clearly limited resource. *What will happen when all domestic resources have been consumed?*

These technologies will impact how North America uses its oil supplies. The discussion throughout this chapter makes it clear that the oil will be more expensive. The projected supply will depend on the price per barrel. Various reports discussed below have the price going from a current figure averaging just over $85 (or over $90) to one around $135 per barrel. It remains to be seen if the economy will hold up with those sorts of price increases.

Unconventional Extraction

Unconventional oil extraction is "industry speak" for new and expensive ways to produce oil. It is an unfortunate choice of words that is a little like referring to a painting as "contemporary art." What is contemporary today will be traditional tomorrow. What is unconventional today may be a standard tomorrow.

The industry currently thinks of conventional oil technology as a hole drilled straight down with a bobbing jack pump on top. If the flow of oil slows down, then you drill a little deeper or you put on a bigger pump to get flow. Most of the oil wells in the U.S. started out this way and still are using that technology. Many of these wells are being drilled to deeper and deeper levels, which add costs while increasing the effort to pump. At the same time, the newer wells are using more and more unconventional methods as the conventional ones decline in production.

Unconventional oil extraction means doing more to produce the oil. That is almost always more expensive. It is sometimes a little more and sometimes a lot more expensive.

The two most widely used and significant developments are *horizontal drilling* and *multilateral drilling*. This means one location can drill into a much wider area. It is what lets offshore oil rigs keep going. It is the big change that is making "fracking" more productive and more widely used.

Of all the new technology, horizontal drilling and multilateral drilling seem to add the least amount of cost. These are technologies that let the wells go deeper and cover a larger area. The wells take a more sophisticated drilling rig. The length of the well is much longer with maximum reach reported up to eight miles. Clearly they are more expensive to drill than a conventional hole straight down. They also require stronger pumps due to the length. However, these are not so much stronger that the increased energy needed for production is showing up in all the industry reports. This adds up to more expense but not on the level of the other unconventional technologies.

Fracking is an abbreviated term for "hydraulic fracturing." It involves dissolving acids, sand and other chemicals in water and pumping it into the wells. This technology has been used a long time in vertically drilled wells and yet it is still considered unconventional technology. The mixture is pumped under high pressure to fracture the rock and the chemicals help by breaking down the minerals that keep the rock intact. The industry claims that there are no documented problems of any significance with this combination of technology.

The fact that the industry says there are no documented problems becomes problematic. There are safety and environmental concerns discussed in Book Three of this series, which is titled *EVs and the Environment*. These concerns have not been addressed to the satisfaction of the scientific community or to policy planners.

The people concerned about this new combination know that a little of something can be good but a lot can do harm. The most familiar example would be a little alcohol helping people relax and a lot of alcohol destroying people's lives. They know that spreading a fertilizer on a garden helps things grow but that too much fertilizer will kill plants. This puts reasonable people in a position where they need clear information to know how to handle either alcohol for enjoyment or fertilizer for their gardens.

This same principle applies to fracking being used at many times the historic rate. There is an increased intensity with the new drilling technology. Both horizontal and multilateral wells result in a much more clustered drilling map than vertical drilling. The higher concentration of wells is then used for more intensive fracking. This needs to be understood more clearly and examined for unintended consequences.

The layout of the wells makes this increasingly clear. The following graphic comes from the Danish Energy Agency and their report titled *Denmark's Producing Fields 2011*. It shows the sort of systematic and comprehensive coverage that is created by these drilling methods. This is happening all over the world and happening quickly. Add to this that chemicals are being injected into this entire area and the concern becomes pretty clear.

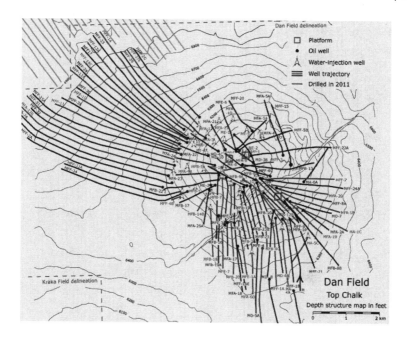

Source: DENMARK'S PRODUCING FIELDS 2011

Who in their right mind would resist wanting to know about massive amounts of chemicals being injected into the ground below our feet? The same thing would apply to having large numbers of holes being drilled below our cities and into the mountains that surround us. There is not enough data about the newer fracking practices and how the areas they are being used in are being impacted. The unintended consequences of this level of activity would happen on what can be a huge scale. The attitude that seems to be coming from the industry is to frack now and ask questions later. Add to that a little of the thought that it is better to apologize later than to ask permission now and we could be heading toward a spectacular problem.

The other aspect of this is how completely the extraction process would pull the resource out of this area. The matrix of horizontal oil wells illustrated above would be pretty effective in extracting almost all of the oil in that formation. At some point, this will have been done to all the known areas for these sorts of resources. *What will be the next step for providing the oil or the energy we need when all of that is used up?*

Heating Things Up

There are two other unconventional ways to extract oil worthy of discussion. One is *thermal extraction* and the other is *surface mining*.

Thermal extraction includes several variations on the idea of pumping heat, usually in the form of steam, into a well or oil deposit. The steam injection method enables the extraction of deposits that are too thick and gooey to pump out easily. This is used in some tight shale situations and in tar sands areas. This involves a costly steam injection system and the oil produced is reported to require more processing to create usable products. The net result is both more expense and higher carbon intensity fuel.

Surface mining is the strip mining process used to pull oil out of sands saturated with tar. Tar Sands processing is discussed in the next chapter. It has similar cost and carbon concerns as thermal extraction.

The world of addiction talks about being in denial of the problems that go along with destructive habits. *Is it possible that the oil industry is walking that path with fracking and tar sands oil production?* When policy-makers have the studies and the science they need then we can all act responsibly.

Future Production and Costs

It is not too difficult to quantify how hard it is to get the oil out of the ground. That runs straight into the question of how much the oil will cost. The next graph shows that clearly. This chart originally had data from 1946 included. Those costs were so consistent that they created a nearly flat line up to the 1970 level. Clearly things have become a lot more volatile since then.

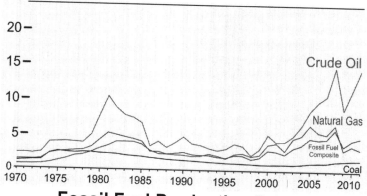

Fossil Fuel Production Prices
Real (2005) Dollars per Million Btu
U.S. Energy Information Administration (EIA), Annual Energy Review 2011

This graph shows that the cost of natural gas production has dropped in recent years. That is the impact of unconventional technology, specifically horizontal drilling combined with fracking. And yet the cost of oil production is not seeing a similar benefit. This may be due to the fundamental difference between a gas and a liquid. A closer look at the specifics of our oil developments may help to understand this better.

The U.S. is one of the most heavily studied and tested oil production areas on the planet. It is not likely that large easily mined oil fields will show up unexpectedly. What is happening is that technology combined with higher prices is making it possible to pump oil from fields that were previously passed over as too expensive to use.

Many of the remaining deposits come with high risks of environmental damage. This information has been separated and will be featured in *Book Three, EVs and the Environment,* for those who have a special interest in it. These environmental risks will, however, involve a price and that price becomes part of the cost of developing the resource. The risks are also associated with a delay in being able to get access to the resource. This issue can be referred to as a *high risk price premium and delays.*

Damage to our land, water and air has a price no matter when it is handled. There is a cost when the damage is allowed to happen and left in place. That cost is losing the use of that land or the degradation of whatever resource is damaged. That cost is paid by future generations.

If the damage is controlled by more expensive production practices, either done voluntarily or due to regulations, then the cost is paid now. That cost is carried by the people benefiting from the production, including both the companies making a profit and the consumer using the resource.

Which approach makes more sense, you paying now or asking your children and grandchildren to pay for you later?

Oil Action in the U.S.

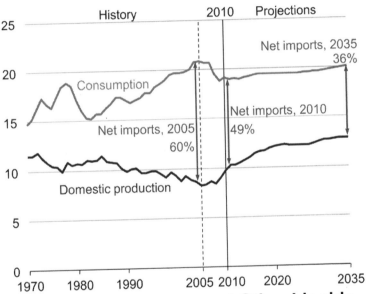

Total U.S. Petroleum and Other Liquids
Production, Consumption, and Net Imports
(Millions of Barrels per Day)

U.S. Energy Information Administration (EIA), Annual Energy Outlook 2012

The graph above shows what has been happening to the production and use of oil in the U.S. as well as what the U.S. Government thinks will happen in the future. The data up to 2010 uses actual numbers, beyond that are projections.

The total U.S. oil production declined steadily from 1975 to 2005. The increase in demand started to be supplied primarily by imported oil from 1975 until recently. The imported oil exceeded the amount produced domestically starting in the mid-90s.

The increase in production that started in 2005 has continued to happen through 2010. It occurred following sharp price increases. The prices in 2010 were three times what they were in 1990. *If it takes nearly a threefold price increase in gasoline to get a little more production, are we in trouble? How much would the price have to go up to get free of imported oil at the current demand?*

The downturn in consumption in 2008-09 is a reflection of the economic problems. There has been a slowing of consumption since, due to both the economic concerns and an increase in efficiency.

This graph is using data that masks the crude oil dependence issue to a certain extent. The category of "petroleum and other liquids" is being used in this graph - instead of crude oil. This category is being used increasingly for government reporting. The designation of "petroleum and other liquids" includes liquid fuels created from renewable sources. It also includes liquids produced from natural gas and from coal. If the chart included only crude oil, then the net imports would have been higher. Crude oil imports would still be over sixty percent of all crude used in this county, having hit a peak of close to seventy percent around 2008.

The increase in production is made possible by the increase in oil prices, which makes it profitable to use oil wells and sources of alternatives to crude that were not usable at lower prices.

This is relevant as there becomes a double count for things like *ethanol*. Ethanol production takes a certain amount of fuel from crude oil. That crude-based fuel is used to create a different fuel (ethanol), that is part of the "other liquid" total. It is a matter of debate as to how much extra fuel is produced from the crude fuel input for ethanol.

Both the crude-based fuel and these other liquid fuels are added to the total. Using crude to make other fuels shifts the percentages imported as well as the total. The math gets confusing and a little weird. The whole thing is a headache waiting to happen and it means that charts like the one above do not give a clear picture of the crude oil imports. That is probably fine as the bigger concern regarding imported oil is the flow of dollars, which can be tracked clearly.

The Gap

The gap between production and consumption is the biggest concern. This is the imported oil gap that is causing the big problems at the national level. It is that gap that connects international events to both your pocketbook and to the security of our country. It is that gap that is causing massive amounts of money to leave our economy and takes our jobs and our tax base with it. The staggering numbers involved with each of these concerns will be discussed, as will the point of view of some of the people who have to handle the consequences.

The nature of this gap is sufficiently important to make sure it is understood clearly. However there are a few more details to cover about this in relation to oil and transportation before we go to the economic and security concerns.

The factors on the U.S. totals graph above are three things that will determine the price we pay for oil. In order for the price to be stable, our consumption would need to be stable, our domestic production would need to keep going, and the cost of imported oil would need to be stable as well. An additional factor not on the graph is the cost of production that would need to stay the same. These factors make up the main elements of supply and demand. As all of these will change, we can expect the price to change.

Our consumption will change because the population will increase. At the current use rate per person, the consumption will go up with the population. Increasing the **efficiency** of our energy use could reduce consumption. Efficiency increases mean better miles per gallon (MPG) for the average vehicle, more people per *vehicle mile traveled* (VMT), as well as better planning and management of transportation. A net reduction in vehicle miles traveled also helps. Efficiency is a key factor in keeping the costs down and getting to oil independence.

A Volt can drive 3,000 miles and more on 10 gallons of gasoline. Yes, it's true; I have done it twice. It's easy. *Does that sound efficient to you?* This reflects the huge energy efficiency advantage to EVs in general. Keep reading to find out more.

The other thing that will reduce consumption is increased cost. People will use less oil by traveling less as the price increases. Traveling less (reducing the VMT) can only go so far before it compromises the quality of life. One thing that will help with this is to find ways to get more of what you need closer to home. Preparing for a reduced travel lifestyle includes building up your local communities. This is referred to as "living locally."

Oil Peaks and Cliffs

The year 1975 has been identified as "the U.S. peak oil production period," which was followed by a predictable decline. *Peak oil* is an idea based on the thinking that we have a specific amount of oil on the planet. It then postulates that our ability to produce oil will reach a maximum and that things are all downhill from there. The problem with this idea is that it is really hard to tell when that will or did happen.

The people who talk in terms of "peak oil" have put forward the idea that the world's oil production will follow a similar decline to the one experienced in the U.S. It makes a nice tidy graph like the decline in U.S. production shown above. The recent development of unconventional extraction techniques is changing how that could play out.

Another idea is that we will use up all the oil in a more dramatic fashion and run into some sort of wall or cliff.

There are varying opinions about how close we are to Peak Oil. There is one group including the Post Carbon Institute that thinks it is in front of us NOW. Some people think it will happen sometime between 2010 and 2025. The English oil executive mentioned above could not tell if or when this was happening. So, *how could people outside the industry possibly come to a definitive conclusion?*

There are others who think that the whole idea of peak oil is a paranoid scheme to justify raising oil prices. While it is certain that energy producers are looking for ways to make more money, it is also generally accepted that new oil and natural gas deposits are not being created. There is no way to replenish what is basically a specific quantity that is currently in existence.

The big concern on the production side has to do with using unconventional oil production technology. These technologies are already increasing U.S. production and it is starting to move above the 1975 "peak." So instead of a slow decline in production, it is full speed ahead.

The concern with the unconventional technology approach is that all of the oil fields may be tapped out as quickly as possible. With the faster and more complete extraction, we are then increasing the possibility of using the oil up at close to the same time.

Are we then trading in a slow decline from an oil peak for the option of running into a cliff of some kind? It could be the kind of "cliff" that a truck would smash into, like a wall created by radical increases in prices. It could be the kind of cliff that a lemming would run over, that represents a steep drop in production.

The development of technology suggests that the concept of peak oil may need revising. Would the peak to be concerned about be a peak in the *per capita rate of oil consumption* rather than a peak in global production? Another Peak that might be suitable to consider is the peak in new discoveries of all potential reserves.

New technology has thwarted the creation of a clear production peak. This is similar to the problem that neo-Malthusian theorists ran into with the concern about population growth.

Malthus was a scientist who had the idea that population growth was limited by the availability of resources. He predicted that population would stop growing as food production and related items became limiting. It sounded like a dire concern when he raised the point over two hundred years ago. It heralded a picture of starvation, disease and war. It came up again in the 1970s with neo-Malthusian ideas that the time was finally upon us. There were around 3.5 billion people on the planet at that point and forty years later we have 7 billion.

The thing that has kept the so-called "Malthusian doom" from showing up has been a combination of new technology used in conjunction with the availability of cheap energy sources. The energy allows the technology to get the job done (creating the resource the people need). Now technology is extending our access to the energy we need, albeit at relatively higher prices.

Robert Malthus did get one thing right and that is the resource cost required to keep lots of people alive and healthy. He missed the part where human ingenuity would help handle that and did not see the cost to other species in that whole process. His theories may become more relevant as the cost of energy increases.

Three Views of the Future

Three recent reports show the range of views that exist today about our oil future. These views range from highly optimistic to serious warnings about the situation. This is a little like "the glass half full or glass half empty" metaphor.

The optimistic view comes from believing science, technology and capitalism will solve things, both in terms of production and consumption efficiency. The serious warnings come from the point of view that we are not paying close enough attention and will drop the ball with human suffering being the result. Both of these points of view have lots of facts to back them up. They both bring value to the table and deserve consideration.

Then there is the middle way. The middle way takes the point of view that the glass is half filled with water and half filled with air. That is a little more on the side of science and a little less connected to the fear of disaster or the unbridled hopes of the optimists.

The following discussion will touch on three reports and the point of view each document represents. The links to these reports at the end of Chapter 2 will allow you to get further information. This may help you see which point of view makes the most sense to you.

Differing Reports

There is a report called the *World Energy Outlook* that suggests the U.S. will in fact increase its production beyond the 1975 peak once again. This could be considered an optimistic view of how all this will work out. This report is produced by the International Energy Agency commissioned in part by the European Union. They summarize the situation as follows:

"By around 2020, the United States is projected to become the largest global oil producer (overtaking Saudi Arabia until the mid-2020s) and starts to see the impact of new fuel-efficiency measures in transport. The result is a continued fall in U.S. oil imports, to the extent that North America becomes a net oil exporter around 2030."

A simple interpretation of that would be: *Problem solved!* Let's get in the SUV and drive a nice long distance!

A more realistic view is tied to the details behind this statement. These include:

- High prices for oil and gasoline to support expensive unconventional extraction
- Ramping up production of all the oil resources discussed in the next chapter
- Using very high levels of energy-efficient technologies, which do not include gas-guzzling SUVs but do include EVs
- The net export horizon of 2030 means more than another decade and a half of continued dependence on imported oil

The prices for oil in the basic projection are up to $135 dollars per barrel by 2030. With recent prices at $87 per barrel, the gasoline price has been around $4.00 in California. That math works out to a U.S. gasoline price of close to $6.50 by and before 2030. This is a really rough estimate and other sources are all over the map.

The report is basically saying that unconventional extraction will go from the current level of just over 800,000 barrels a day to well over 10 million barrels a day in less than fifteen years. This would have to happen while the conventional oil fields are keeping up a reasonable level of production as well. Not everyone is confident that this will or can happen.

The production rates are going up already. The part in question is how much they will increase and how long they would stay at the higher levels.

The *World Energy Outlook* report is significantly different in its projections than the reports from the U.S. Government. The Annual Energy Outlook 2012 from the U.S. Department of Energy has a number of different projections. The last graph above showing the U.S. total production and consumption is from the Annual Energy Outlook report from 2012. It shows what they were projecting one year ago. They project a continued need for oil imports at more than thirty-five percent of our consumption.

The more recent version of that last report released in 2013 has changes as illustrated in the updated graph below. This graph is the updated version of the one shown above that has the more suitable title, *Total U.S. petroleum and other liquids production, consumption, and net imports.* This shows that the projected consumption has been reduced and the projected production has been increased. Both of these are reasonably consistent with the information about new technologies. They also represent an acknowledgment of the position taken by the *World Energy Outlook Report.*

What a difference a year makes!

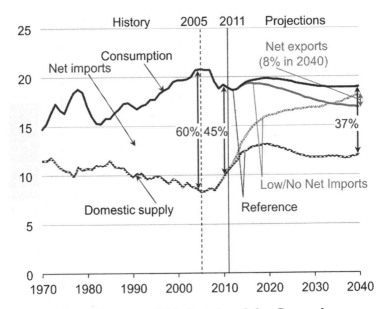

Net Share of U.S. Liquids Supply
in Two Cases, 1970 to 2040 (Million Barrels per Day)
U.S. Energy Information Administration (EIA), Annual Energy Outlook 2013

This updated graph also has two items added to the projections. These lines are labeled Low/No Net Imports (the lighter grey lines). One of these shows a huge increase in production as the result of the new technology. The other line shows a substantial additional reduction in consumption. These both look more like what the World Energy Outlook Report describes. Adding these two new lines to the graph gives all of us a good visual aid to evaluate the optimistic view of the World Energy Outlook compared to the more conservative view of the Annual Energy Outlook.

A first reaction is that the optimistic changes are less consistent with recent trends than the more conservative view. Then again, perhaps they have new data that really has changed that much in one or two years!

A second reaction is to wonder exactly how the U.S. will reduce its consumption. What will the consequences be of that happening? How can that be possible in the face of increased population?

Finally, the huge uptick in oil production that is in the prediction would have major economic benefits to our country. That level of economic improvement would increase the income of people in the U.S., which that has historically translated into increased use of fuel. Would it really be possible to reduce consumption in times of an economic boom? Chances are that both of these hoped for changes would not happen at the same time.

The Post Carbon Institute has responded to these and other reports as well as to the politically simple idea of the solution being to "drill baby drill." This report has a more cautious view that comes with more of a warning tone. Their report is actually called *"Drill, Baby, Drill: Can Unconventional Fuels Usher in a New Era of Energy Abundance?"* Here is what the executive summary from that report by J. David Hughes has to say:

"The U.S. cannot drill and frack its way to 'energy independence.' At best, shale gas, tight oil, tar sands, and other unconventional resources provide a temporary reprieve from having to deal with the real problems: fossil fuels are finite, and production of new fossil fuel resources tends to be increasingly expensive and environmentally damaging. Fossil fuels are the foundation of our modern global economy, but continued reliance on them creates increasing risks for society that transcend our economic, environmental, and geopolitical challenges. The best responses to this conundrum will entail a rethink of our current energy trajectory.

"Unfortunately, the 'drill, baby, drill' rhetoric in recent U.S. elections belies any understanding of the real energy problems facing society. The risks of ignoring these energy challenges are immense. Developed nations like the United States consume (on a per capita basis) four times as much energy as China and seventeen times as much as India. Most of the future growth in energy consumption is projected to occur in the developing world. Constraints in energy supply are certain to strain future international relations in unpredictable ways and threaten U.S. and global economic and political stability. The sooner the real problems are recognized by political leaders, the sooner real solutions to our long-term energy problem can be implemented."

So here you have well-researched reports coming from well-considered groups that ended up with different conclusions from looking at the same or similar sets of facts. Again, the three reports involved are:

1. *The World Energy Outlook Report* from the E.U.-based International Energy Agency (I.E.A.)
2. *The Annual Energy Outlook* from the U.S. Department of Energy (E.I.A.)
3. *Drill Baby Drill* from the Post Carbon Institute

Each of them sounds reasonable when you read through the reports. *How is it that they come to such different conclusions?* The answer has to do with the underlying assumptions each group is working with and the weight they give to different sets of information.

Here are the big differences between these reports:

COMPARISON OF MAJOR OIL OUTLOOKS

Report Name	U.S. Total Oil Consumption	Domestic Oil Production	Oil Imports by 2030
World Energy Report	Declines	Growth spurt followed by a steady increase	Imports less than Exports
Annual Energy Outlook	Grows, then settle back to current levels	Growth spurt followed by a decline	37% of Total Demand
Drill Baby Drill	No Projection	Declines	Unsustainable

The assumptions and weight being assigned to the data focus on some key areas. Here are a few questions for you to think about that relate to this:

- *How long will unconventional extraction produce high volume results?*
- *How will the environmental consequences impact the extraction and its costs?*
- *How would an increase in the price of oil reduce the quality of life in the U.S. or in Europe?*
- *How will the imbalance of energy consumption between different countries influence global stability?*

- *How will countries that import a lot of oil, pay for that oil?*
- *What will the U.S. and Europe produce that the oil-producing countries will want in exchange for oil?*
- *What will the oil-producing countries want in exchange for oil if we do not produce goods or services that they want?*
- *How quickly will we adopt the energy-efficient technologies needed to control the increase in oil demand?*

You can sidestep all of these questions very simply. Just stop guzzling gas and drive on domestically produced electricity! Heck, then you can skip the next few discussions completely and focus on how to use these great vehicles.

It would help most people to get a better understanding of our energy future if they have some more data to work with. The following discussion will help provide some important points for consideration. See if any of this suggests a more secure future by continuing our dependence oil or by relying on domestically produced electricity.

Links on North American Oil

The links at the end of Chapter 2, *King of the Road*, cover the main sources of data for this current chapter (including the three reports). Here are a few more select items.

The National Academies Press
www.nap.edu/openbook.php?record_id=12794&page=1

Additional Links
www.naturalgas.org/overview/unconvent_ng_resource.asp
www.nytimes.com/2011/06/26/us/26gas.html?pagewanted=all&_r=1&
www.capp.ca
www.dnrc.mt.gov

The Peak and Decline of World Oil and Gas Production
www.peakoil.net/publications/the-peak-and-decline-of-world-oil-and-gas-production

Chapter 4

U.S. Oil Deposits

There is another not very well-kept Energy Secret. It is more of a common sense idea that most people just do not want to think about. Here it is:

Energy (Not-so) Secret
The most expensive oil deposits have been left for last.

A closer look at the three most promising sources of U.S. oil will highlight this idea. These are the ones with the possibility of increased production over the next ten to fifteen years. Canadian tar sands are a North American prospect too, so that will also be considered and is listed last below.

- North Slope Oil in Alaska
- Offshore Oil on the Pacific Coast and in the Gulf of Mexico
- Tight Oil Shale around the country
- Tar Sands from Canada

All four of these have been left for development until now for one very simple reason. It *costs more* to extract the oil from these sources than from the traditional ones. The vast majority of oil resources that can be extracted by conventional methods have been and continue to be worked. Those are the ones that have been declining in production. Many of those are now being converted to unconventional methods of extraction, which means higher costs.

There is one part of the increased cost that goes beyond the money involved. It is the amount of energy it takes to get the energy out of the ground. An oil gusher from back in the day produced the energy without requiring even the energy to pump it. These days even conventional wells with one hole and a pump on top are taking more energy to suck the oil out. These wells are going deeper and deeper, so that takes ever more energy to get the oil to the surface. The unconventional technologies described in the previous chapter all consume increasing amounts of energy.

The energy used to extract the oil has been analyzed by the Energy Technology Systems Analysis Program (ETSAP), which is part of the International Energy Agency (I.E.A.). Below is a quote from their 2010 report called *Unconventional Oil & Gas Production.*

"The energy input used in conventional oil and natural gas production is about 6% of the energy produced. To produce unconventional oil and gas resources the energy required in the process is much more."

The energy required to extract the oil is a separate consideration because it creates a self-perpetuating spiraling of the costs. When energy prices go up, the more expensive energy becomes profitable. If it takes a lot of energy to produce the more expensive oil, then the cost of production will get more expensive. The more expensive energy will in turn drive up the price of energy.

This is a little abstract, so let's create two examples to show how this works. One example would be if the energy in one barrel of oil can produce twenty barrels from an oil field. That is a five percent energy usage. If this were to happen, recently - when oil was priced at $80 per barrel - that means the energy used to produce each of the twenty barrels would be $4.

The second example would be if the energy in one barrel of oil can produce four barrels from an oil field. That is about a 25 percent energy usage. A little math and we find out the energy cost would be five times as much for the second example. If we use the $80 per barrel price then the energy used to produce each barrels would cost $20.00. If this second example is in fifteen years from now when the oil is costing $135 per barrel - it would be even more expensive. The energy cost at that point would be $33.75 a barrel produced. That is almost ten times the dollar amount than when oil was produced at cheaper energy costs.

This shows us how important the energy used in production is to the ability to use the oil affordably. The example shows the difference between five percent and twenty-five percent. That may seem like a big range but it is actually less than the numbers reported by the Energy Technology Systems Analysis Program (ETSAP) report, *Unconventional Oil & Gas Production 2011.* Here is what they report as the percentages required.

OIL EXTRACTION ENERGY USAGE
As a percentage of the energy value produced

Conventional Oil	6%
Extra Heavy Oil	20 – 25%
Oil Sand	30%
Oil Shale	30%

Source: Energy Technology Systems Analysis Program (ETSAP),
Unconventional Oil & Gas Production 2011

The price of energy is one thing that will determine how quickly the price for gas in dollars will be impacted. Sources of oil that use less energy will stay more affordable. As the price goes up, sources that use more energy will price themselves into less profitable production.

That has been happening since the beginning of commerce and it means that the low energy-consuming sources have been used up first. These would be the oil equivalent of low hanging fruit.

Our ability to get reasonably priced fuel will depend on the extent that our fuel is in this spiral. A description of the oil reserves we are using will help you understand how much energy is being used for production. That is one key factor in how stable the prices will be and how quickly the fuel prices will rise.

Too Expensive to Consider

Some potential sources of fuel are so energy and capital intensive to extract that they are not being used. They may never be used to their capacity because of this spiral.

There is one reservoir of energy deposits that demonstrates this well. It is too expensive to be seriously considered. It is the *Oil Shale Deposits*. This is different from the Tight Shale Oil story discussed below.

Oil Shale is a misnomer. It does not even include actual oil. Rather, it contains "oil-like" deposits that some people refer to as unfinished oil. There are two ways to use it to keep our economy going. One way is to dig the rock up, crush it into small pieces, and cook it at 700 degrees or more for a long time. The other way is to heat big areas of rock in place and then use fracking technology to extract the oil. The heating part is needed to turn the organic hydrocarbons into something like conventional crude.

The industry has not figured out how to strip mine and cook rock economically, let alone handle the environmental concerns with doing this to areas of scenic natural beauty. They have the technology to do the cooking onsite. This includes controlling the water by freezing an area around the extraction site to keep the fracking water in place. They just haven't out figured out how to do that economically yet.

What that means in the big picture is that the price for oil would have to be so strong that it would be worthwhile to go after these resources. That becomes a look at the future and gives you an idea of what the energy extraction will look like generations from now. Putting that sort of destruction as far in the future as possible is one reason to increase transportation efficiencies with electric vehicles.

There are, however, a number of ways to keep our oil production going that are economically viable. There are some environmental impacts that go along with each of these and those are discussed in Book Three, *EVs and the Environment.* Even if you are not particularly concerned about the environmental impacts, the concerns will mean two things. One is a longer development cycle and the other is the possibility of higher costs of production. Both of which will impact how much you pay at the pump.

U.S. "Oil Plays"

Here is a look at the top three oil prospects within the U.S.A. and what promise they hold for volume and cost. The oil industry calls each new development an "oil play" or a "gas play." Who knew they were having so much fun?

North Slope Oil in Alaska
The story of the oil in Alaska is a microcosm of the story for the country. The graph below shows what has happened to this fabled production area. The areas that have been authorized for production have been tapped out using conventional methods, as well as a lot of horizontal and multilateral drilling. The production in those areas can be extended with other unconventional methods. There are also additional areas that can be brought into production that are not shown on this graph. The graph includes both crude oil and natural gas liquids (NFL) that are prized fuels.

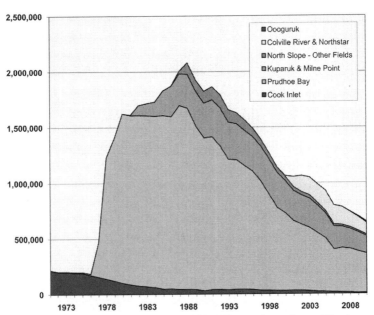

Alaska's Average Daily Production Rate
Oil and Natural Gas Liquids (Barrels per Day)
AOGCC, February 10, 2011

This graph is typical of many oil fields. It shows a somewhat dramatic peak oil curve. The rapid buildup, followed by the relatively steep decline is the sort of cycle that the Post Carbon group is concerned about. That group is concerned that the rapid decline side of this is becoming increasingly rapid, meaning the new technology will diminish the production more quickly.

A 2008 report by the National Energy Technology Laboratory of the Department of Energy (DOE) examines the future of the area. The report is called *Alaska North Slope Oil and Gas, A Promising Future or an Area in Decline?* It has the following projection for the expanded area.

"The forecasts of economically recoverable oil and gas additions, including reserves growth in known fields, is 35 to 36 billion barrels of oil and 137 trillion cubic feet of gas."

That is enough oil to supply the United States for about five years at current consumption rates. It would require opening up a new area (ANWR #1002) for production and takes into account using unconventional extraction methods. It also calls for some offshore drilling in Arctic waters. The extraction methods may have improved since then and that would increase the reserves available. The oil prices may go even higher so that might add more to the proven supply.

Part of what would be required to make this happen is a new natural gas pipeline from the North Slope to the Pacific Ocean. The natural gas pipeline would allow extraction of the natural gas at the same time as the oil and that improves the viability of the whole process.

The production graph above shows how an oil field plays out. The length of time for full production varies, as does the rate of decline. This is a reasonably typical graph and there are many similar ones available from the various links in this book. The length of production and the rate of decline are key elements in the different points of view given by the three reports discussed in the last chapter.

Offshore Oil

The oil platforms offshore along the Pacific Coast and in the Gulf of Mexico have experienced real disasters that had huge impacts on our marine life, beaches, fisheries and the people in local communities. BP's Horizon well blowout in the Gulf of Mexico keeps this concern clear in our minds. The BOP Horizon oil disaster showed us three things.

1. There is a huge oil supply under pressure in the offshore oil wells.
2. The cost of tapping that supply safely is complex and more expensive than the oil companies wanted to deal with before the incident.
3. There is a huge potential to bring great harm to many people and the environment.

These three factors net out to a large potential supply of oil, provided enough money is spent to extract it safely; in other words, it brings an expensive supply.

There is another area that is prime territory for drilling oil offshore. It is off the northern coast of this continent in Alaska in Arctic waters, as mentioned above.

Tight Oil

The other source for oil that is already being expanded rapidly is the *tight oil deposits,* which are actual reservoirs of oil commonly found in shale around the country. It is hard to get the oil out of most shale oil deposits. The more easily extracted parts have been tapped long ago, particularly in North America. This means that the oil producers are turning to various intensive mining practices to get the oil out. These include fracking as well as horizontal and multilateral drilling. All of these techniques are more expensive and have lower long-term production than the traditional methods.

The big success stories for tight oil are found in North Dakota at the Bakken Shale formation and in Texas at the Eagle Ford Shale deposits. There is a long list of names of other tight oil deposits around the country. The production from these moved into the 800,000 barrels per day category in late 2011/early 2012. There are solid industry projections that show this doubling by

2015. The Post Carbon Institute report is less optimistic based on their views on rapid production decreases for new oil plays.

The Monterey Shale deposits in California are being boosted in production using the unconventional technologies. This deposit runs down the Central Valley and is extracted heavily in the Bakersfield area. It also goes down the Pacific Coast from Monterey to Los Angeles.

The addition of the new drilling technology combined with hydraulic fracturing could double the current oil production outlook of these areas.

There are three big differences between the North Dakota and Texas production areas and the Monterey Shale areas. The first difference is that only one of them sits beneath the major watershed for one of the most significant food growing areas on the planet. That same watershed provides drinking water for the Central Valley and both Los Angeles and the San Francisco Bay Area.

The watershed is experiencing increasingly chronic water shortages. The water needed to do the fracking would add significant demand to those conditions. The watershed is being drilled to ever deeper levels to get the water.

There is no data about the point at which the fracking operations will result in contamination of that watershed needed by local farms and cities. The fracking water is reported to be accumulated in surface ponds and then removed from the site for disposal. This raises the question of how they dispose of the water. Municipal water systems are not configured to deal with the chemical composition and contamination found in fracking waste water. Every fracking operation would need to have a disposal system for this water and there are no reports about how this is being handled.

The surface collection ponds present the possibility of surface water contamination and water injected under the ground can contaminate ground water. The water used in fracking is disposed of, in part, by injecting it into oil shale and sometimes even deeper. There is little known about how that may or may not result in intrusions into the aquifers that feed our ground water and municipal water supplies.

The second difference for the Monterey Shale option is that some part of this area means offshore drilling. It also means intensified drilling along the shoreline. This is already a problem in Hermosa Beach. *How ready are we to deal with all that?*

The final difference has to do with the underlying geology. The fields in places like North Dakota and Texas are all in areas where the oil deposits are more or less flat. That is to say, they are at the same depth below the surface. This is due to and accompanied by a relatively low concentration of earthquake faults. This allows reasonably easy and cost-effective horizontal drilling.

This is in sharp contrast to the Monterey Shale. This shale has been subject to high levels of geologic movement and folding. The deposits are far from being flat. This makes tapping the resource more challenging. They are also in areas with prolific earthquake faults. That raises questions of seismic stability as well as challenges to do with well site stability and migration of fracking and other fluids.

The fracking process involves fracturing the rock removing large amounts of crude. Removing the crude creates room for the fractured rock to shift, hence the well site stability concern. Replacing the crude with contaminated water is one option to help with this. This water could be able to escape the fractured oil field. Contaminated water is also disposed of by injecting it into rock layers even deeper than the shale oil. That is closer to where the earthquake faults are located. Water acts as a lubricant so the whole process breaks up and weakens the rock near earthquake faults that have been lubricated by water.

This sounds serious but there is little if any data to evaluate how serious it is. Furthermore there would be a need to evaluate this on a case-by-case basis in areas with the diverse geology like that found in California. The fracking is going forward quickly and extensively anyway.

These differences will raise major concerns and rightfully so.

Which is more essential, oil or water?

What about oil versus increased earthquake activity?

When major concerns are associated with any industry, it means higher costs and longer development times. That is just what it takes to protect the interests of all people concerned.

Tight oil will bring in a good part of the daily production needs. It may get to the four or five fold production increases that are being discussed. That would put it close to 4 million barrels per day out of the almost 20 million we are currently using. This is one area of projection that varies between the three oil energy reports discussed in Chapter 3.

All the reports agree that oil from all of these U.S.-based sources will be more expensive. They agree that it will only be produced if the price of gas is high enough to make production profitable.

Canadian Tar Sands

The Canadian reserves shown in the graph for North American Proven Oil Reserves at the beginning of the previous chapter are primarily in Tar Sands. The availability of that is due to the new economics of both high prices and reduced costs that make tar sands profitable. In 2002, Canada had a reported proven reserve of around 5 billion barrels. In 2003, that number jumped to 180 billion barrels (the number in 2012 is 173 BB). Hello Tar Sands Oil!

The resource is in Canada and yet it is talked about as if it will solve the domestic supply for the U.S. At least it is North America "domestic." Canada has been a good neighbor and any economic prosperity in Canada has translated into a benefit for the U.S. That makes them an international source that works better than sources from people who disdain or avoid doing business with the United States.

One drawback to the resource being in Canada is the pipeline part. That oil will travel across the middle of our country as a very crude product in a very long pipe. The pipe is called the XL Pipeline and there are many people concerned about the consequences of that project. These factors bring this close to home.

It would be nice if this source would solve our need for cheap oil. However, that might not be the case for a whole lot of reasons.

One big reason is that the cheapest way to get oil out of the ground is to strip mine it. That means turning large tracks of land upside down and hauling major amounts of material away.

That material includes lots of sand and clay all mixed in with a really nasty tar-like material (*bitumen* by name). The mess has to be separated, which means you then have to do something with dirty sand and clay and a heavy thick petroleum product. The sand and clay will go back to where it came from, with substantial tar contamination. Eventually it will be used to try to reclaim the land.

The land has not been reclaimed to any real degree yet. It is reported to be a ten-year process or is that a forty-year process! *What will the reclamation cost be for doing that and will it actually ever get done? How much money is being set aside and expensed out now to do that work? What will that mean to the price of that source of energy five years from now and beyond?*

While the potential resource is huge, only about ten percent of it is close to the surface. The rest of it will need to be extracted with even more expensive methods than strip mining. That would involve thermal extraction, which is one of the unconventional technologies discussed in the previous chapter.

The land destroyed by mining is only part of the added expense. Both the extraction and onsite processing of the tar is using a huge amount of water. The tar is full of all sorts of impurities and many of them are hazardous. These are ending up in the water being used. The water is turned into a mix of all sorts of chemicals. There are so many chemicals that the industry is still figuring out what they are. That water is accumulating in huge "settling ponds" the size of small cities. These will need to be dealt with sooner or later - or not. Either way, there are costs down the road that will hit the price at the pump.

Tar sands extraction is expensive in part because it involves tar, not oil. Tar is far from being like the stuff that goes into a car engine. Getting the sand and clay out is one step and then there is doing what it takes to get it to move in a pipeline. It is so thick and heavy that it is tough to make it even begin to flow. This nasty stuff does not move through pipes well. It has to be either chemically split or thinned out. Thinning tar out means adding oil-based solvents or thinners. They have to extract the tar, extract or refine the solvents, and then heat up the tar to dissolve the solvents into it just to get it all into a pipe

The oil refineries are not set up to handle such heavy thick material. The material has to be fixed before the standard refining will work. This means doing what is known as upgrading it to the crude oil standards. This involves a set of processes that are referred to as *Hydro-processing* and are all done at temperatures upwards of 300 degrees Celsius.

Refining the material in the increased quantities is also posing a problem. Doing it in Alberta where it is extracted is a problem. It is really cold up there. The ground freezes and is unstable at best. Putting in foundations for refineries is really expensive and running a refinery in such cold temperatures would be costly as well. The engineers involved talk about how the pilings pop out of the ground when it freezes. Tar gets even tougher to work with when it is cold.

So they want to pipe the material over a 1,000 miles south to Texas. That would be a big long and expensive pipe. They are using trains for that purpose as well. Talk about a train wreck waiting to happen.

Unfortunately the fourth such wreck happened as this book was being prepared for market. A train, loaded with as much as 2 million gallons of crude oil, crashed into a downtown area in the Canadian town of Lac-Mégantic, Thirty buildings were completely destroyed, with 24 confirmed dead and a further 26 missing but presumed deceased. The amount of oil released into a nearby River is not fully disclosed.

Sometimes a humorous prediction can be no fun to have come true. This concern is now clearly on the table with a large tragedy to show the way.

Does any of this sound cheap to you? It is better than shale oil, but that is not saying much.

Tar sands are a good example of the reasons why the World Energy Outlook 2012 report covers its back with statements like:

"Policy-makers looking for simultaneous progress towards energy security, economic and environmental objectives are facing increasingly complex – and sometimes contradictory – choices."

The global situation is part of that complex and sometimes contradictory mess. This report comes off a little less optimistic on that level, as the following statement shows.

"Taking all new developments and policies into account, the world is still failing to put the global energy system onto a more sustainable path."

Clearly there are very real and basic concerns about oil. These concerns will target your personal pocket-book and they are creating huge challenges for our country. The challenges are impacting our national and personal security, as well as our jobs and national economy.

Links on U.S. Oil Deposits

The links at the end of Chapter 2, *King of the Road*, cover the main sources of data for this current chapter. Here are a few more select items.

National Energy Technology Laboratory
www.netl.doe.gov
www.netl.doe.gov/technologies/oil-gas/publications/brochur
es/Microhole2006_Mar.pdf

Energy Technology Systems Analysis Program (ETSAP)
www.etsap.org
www.iea-etsap.org/web/E-TechDS/PDF/P02-Uncon%20oil
&gas-GS-gct.pdf

Alaska North Slope Oil
www.doa.alaska.gov/ogc/ActivityCharts/Production/110210
HistoricalProd1958-2010.pdf

Chapter 5

Jobs and the Economy

These are challenging economic times. The great recession has taken its toll all over the world. The net result is still being felt in Europe and North America. Europe is doing everything it can to keep the Union going with one debt crisis after another. The United States is expanding its debt at the fastest rate in history, and it is still not able to create the needed jobs. The jobs being created pay less than ever, with people's incomes shrinking as a result. That could be called *job deflation* or *income deflation*. Some people are doing super well, while most people are seeing their incomes drop or have trouble finding an income.

What does that have to do with electric vehicles?

The EV Connection

The connection is that EVs help to stop the drain of money out of the national economy of all net oil-importing countries. Questions about that economic drain include:

How has and does that petro-dollar drain impact your economic well-being?

How does the drain influence your ability to make the money for a good quality of life?

Driving an EV means you are buying fuel that is domestically produced or produced by a close neighbor. It means that you are keeping your hard-earned money in your area so that your neighbors can keep their jobs. They keep their jobs, and in turn, you have a chance to get some of your money back through your business or your place of employment.

The money spent for oil-based fuels leaves at the local level, at the state level and at the national level. It is leaving to pay for oil at truly monumental rates. That money goes out and is not coming back easily. It is shifting the economic strength to the countries that are on the receiving end of all that oil money.

The drain of money that is leaving the economies of the U.S., the E.U. and Japan has not been given a lot of attention in the discussion of the recession and the slow recovery. It has become the elephant in the room that no one wants to talk about. Well, I like elephants and have no problem talking about them. In this situation, there are several elephants involved. One is called *Oil and Such*, one is called *Cars and Parts*, and one is called *Chinese Consumer Goods*. In addition, there is the baby of the group which we will call a *Little of This and That*.

The category Oil and Such includes oil, gas, petroleum and coal. The category Cars and Parts includes components, chassis, and sub-assemblies that supply domestic production, as well as substantial numbers of fully assembled finished vehicles. This category also includes replacement parts and some of the imported components that feed so-called assembly plants. These plants are where imported components are added to domestically produced parts and turned into full vehicles. These are the trade categories that would dominate most oil-importing countries. It might be worthwhile to look at similar numbers for any country or even a state that is important to you. This would be particularly true for the debt-burdened countries in Europe that have no oil of their own.

The discussion can start with describing just how big these elephants really are. Here are some numbers to help describe the size of these as they show up in the U.S. economy as the main example. Each of these elephants represents money leaving the U.S. economy. There is a domestic level of production in each of these categories that is in addition to the money that leaves the economy. When money leaves an economy to buy goods or services that is considered a negative balance of trade for those goods. When a specific country has an overall negative balance of trade, it is an indication of that being a transfer of wealth to the countries that provide the goods and services.

The following graph shows the total net balance of trade for the years from 2000 to 2009. It then breaks things down for each of the big old elephants. Yes, they do all add up to the total of all money leaving the U.S.

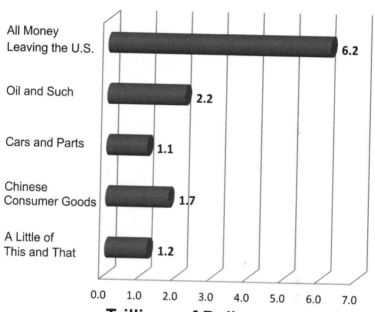

Trillions of Dollars
Leaving the U.S. Economy
over the first ten years of this century
Data Source: Office of Trade and Industry Information,
Manufacturing and Services, International Trade Administration

Clearly the biggest amount of money is tied to the elephant called Oil and Such, as well as to its smaller relative, Cars and Parts.

Right now, these two elephants seem to be the biggest categories for most countries. The tables in the previous chapters on the global oil supply would guide you to find both the countries with the Oil and Such variety of concern and the countries that are gaining the benefits of us having this problem.

A trillion dollars here and two trillion there and pretty soon there is some real money involved. *Just how much does this represent?*

It is really hard to get a perspective on these sorts of numbers. Yet, without some sort of perspective, it is hard to know just how much these concerns are related to our daily lives. The two trillion dollars sent out of our economy for oil can be put in perspective with a few choice numbers for comparison.

- Two trillion dollars can pay for the entire economic activity of California for over a year. There would be enough left over to buy a whole city.

- The two trillion dollars in oil money is enough to make two million millionaires. Those millionaires will now live and pay taxes in another country.

- The oil money was just over one-third of all the money that left our economy in the first decade of this century.

- Over the period from 1990 to 1999, $550 billion left the economy to pay for Oil and Such. The $2.2 trillion is four times bigger than that amount for the same number of years.

- The country spent as much on imported oil in just TWO years (2007-08) as it did in the ten years from 1990 to 1999!

Another thing that might put this into perspective is the timing of this and how this has changed over recent history. The U.S. has not always had a negative balance of trade. It was actually a positive trade balance until 1982. That corresponds to the time right after the domestic oil production reached its peak in the mid-70s. The start of the negative balance of trade in 1982 also corresponds to the start of an increase in another part of our economic activity, as will be discussed in a moment. Here is what has happened since 1982:

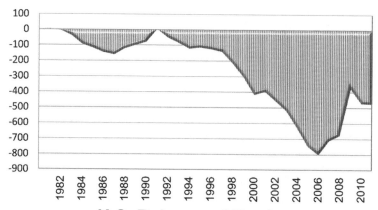

U.S. Balance of Trade
(Dollars Lost in Billions)
Data Source: U.S. Bureau of Economic Analysis,
U.S. International Transactions

The U.S. economy has huge holes in it that are draining money and jobs out of the country. Could money leaving our economy at such a staggering rate be the underlying reason our economy is not recovering and one reason why we are not creating new jobs?

If you want to make more jobs, the classic answer is to pump more stimulus money into the economy. That approach worked for many decades and helped build the country. The approach is still working; it is just not working for the people in the United States and much of the E.U. How can this approach create domestic jobs when a large part of the stimulus money leaves the country really quickly? The net result is that jobs are created overseas with our trading partners - China, Canada and Mexico being the top three major beneficiaries.

It becomes more likely that our balance of trade is at the root of our problems when you compare these numbers to what we produce in total goods and services. That information is available as the Gross Domestic Product (GDP) figures provided by the U.S. Department of Commerce. Here are a couple of numbers that show the comparison:

GROSS DOMESTIC PRODUCT for 2008
(Trillions of Dollars)

United States GDP	14.2
California GDP	1.8

Source: Bureau of Economic Analysis, National Income and
Product Accounts Table

With $6.2 trillion leaving our economy in ten years, that works out to be over forty percent of the money needed to buy everything produced in our country in one year. It is more than enough money to buy all the goods and services produced for over three years in California. Just how much money has to leave our country before it has the sort of impact like the great recession?

The housing problem has taken the brunt of the blame for the recession. People got to the point where they could not pay their mortgages so the house of cards came down. Toward the end of this chapter we will explore the question - Did that happen because the money they needed to pay the mortgage went to pay for Oil and Such or one of the other elephants in the economy?

The year 2008 is chosen for the Gross Domestic Product data above for several reasons. It was close to the point of peak economic activity, so this represents a high point. It is also the year that is **CLOSE** to the maximum negative balance of trade, as well as being the year the economy took a nosedive in the last half. Are these connected by coincidences or is this a matter of cause and effect?

The peak in the **TOTAL** negative balance of trade actually happened in 2006, as shown above. The peak that did occur in 2008 was the money spent to import **Oil and Such.** Imported oil is the main thing that caused the transfer of wealth for oil and such to go from $250 billion in 2006 to close to $400 billion in 2008. When the economy took a nosedive, then so did the total negative balance of trade for Oil and Such in 2009. Here is what that looks like:

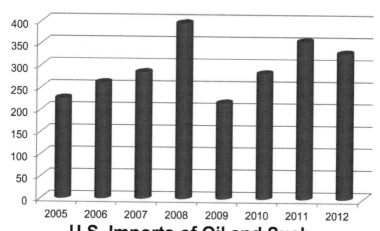

U.S. Imports of Oil and Such
Oil, Gas, Petroleum and Coal (Billions of Dollars)
Data Source: Office of Trade and Industry Information, Manufacturing and
Services, International Trade Administration

Once again, the question of coincidence versus *cause and effect* comes to mind. *Is it possible that the huge amount of money leaving our economy would cause a collapse or some sort of domestic recession?* If it is cause and effect, then the recent increases in imported Oil and Such may have further pending consequences.

There is report from a group called the Blue Green Alliance called *Gearing Up, Smart Standards Create Good Jobs Building Cleaner Cars*. The report supports the idea that oil is a cause of recessions. It looks only at the price of oil and not at the trade balance. The report has a great graph called *Oil Price Spikes, the Incidence of Economic Recessions*. That report shows a very close connection between oil prices and economic recessions in the U.S. The link at the end of this chapter will let you access that graph.

An Amazing Economy

It is pretty amazing that the U.S. Economy has recovered from the recession. It is able to go on while our family of elephants is going on having so much activity. *How can we buy more stuff than we produce in such high quantities without totally going upside down?*

If each of us did that in our personal lives, we would go broke really quickly. That is to say we would be going into debt so quickly that the banks would catch up to us and put a stop to that. After all, *where is all that money coming from?*

The key word here is ***debt***. It has a lot to do with personal debt, but it also has to do with government debt. The federal government goes into debt to try to stimulate jobs and the economy. Instead of creating jobs, the debt is putting money in the economy but then it goes straight to pay for Oil and Such and the rest of the negative balance of trade elephant family.

A look at the numbers will show one reason the money is available to support the negative balance of trade. Here is a graph of the history of the level of federal government debt:

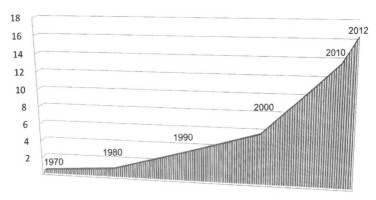

Total U.S. Federal Debt
at the End of Each Decade plus EOY 2012
(Trillions of Dollars)
Data Source: U.S. Treasury Direct

What is 16 TRILLION dollars? It is enough to buy all the goods and services produced in the U.S. in 2008 with 2 trillion to spare. At least this part of things is being discussed by the media and the political system.

Not only is this massive amount of debt troublesome. In addition, the fact that it continues to increase at ever faster rates is pretty serious. The total debt increased by almost 3 trillion from

2010 to 2012, which is ***over twice the rate*** of the previous decade. Combine that with a jobless recovery and there are real questions about where all that money has gone.

There are two other related concerns waiting in the wings. The first concern has to do with how much this huge debt is costing us. Right now, the interest on this debt is not at a very high rate, based on the Treasury bond and related markets. The interest rates controlled by the government are as close to zero as they can be (as of this writing). This means the government has a lot of reasons (16 trillion and counting) to keep that interest rate as close to zero as possible. This debt is pretty much a variable rate loan. The question is - *What happens to this picture if interest rates start to go up?*

The second concern has to do with the international status of the dollar. For the last fifty years, the dollar has been the most trusted currency in the world. It is used to conduct over sixty percent all international business. That includes all the oil transactions and is more than any other currency. Economists talk about this as the dollar being the dominant *reserve currency*. That is why we have been able to produce more and more dollars without having big problems. There has been a hungry world waiting to use the relatively stable currency to conduct business.

The currency has been stable because it was managed beautifully through 1980 and reasonably up to around 2000 when the increase in debt took off. Then the debt escalated again after 2008, starting with the bank, and related to the "too big to fail" bailouts. In recent years, the U.S. and other countries have been using debt to pay off debt at increasing rates. We are buying things we are paying for by printing money. *How long will that continue before the dollar becomes less valuable and our costs for imports of all kinds take off?*

Countries all over the world are starting to take measures to side-step using the dollar to do business. This means that they are cutting the need to own dollars and reducing the demand accordingly. You know what happens when demand drops for anything. The value goes down with the demand. In the case of the dollar, that means the price of things like oil going up faster.

The media is not talking so much about either the degradation of the dollar by our debt or about the money being paid out for the family of trade deficit elephants. This level of economic analysis does not seem to be reflected in any of the economic reports on energy.

When you add the increased cost to get oil out of the ground to the international economic uncertainty of our handling of the dollar, the combined effect makes the future cost of oil seriously problematic.

Is the debt and trade balance relationship another coincidence? The federal government goes deeply into debt at the same time that the balance of trade goes seriously upside down. A look at these two numbers side-by-side will show just how closely these two coincide.

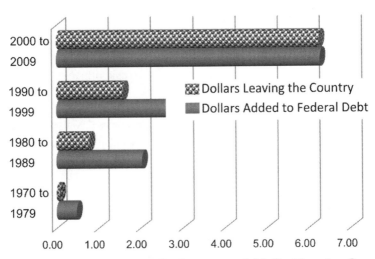

Comparing the Balance of U.S. Trade & Total Federal Debt
(Trillions of Dollars)

The Federal Debt increased by close to the same number of dollars as our balance of trade deficit for the first time in history, right when the country ended up in economic trouble. That trouble is stabilized by increasing the rate of our debt creation, which is otherwise known as using debt to pay our bills.

Is the money that goes with the increased debt what has allowed us to buy the Oil and Such? Is the extra stimulus enough to avoid another downturn or are we just buying time?

The money used for Oil and Such is real business sent overseas. The jobs and tax revenues have gone with that money. That leaves the U.S. without the income tax and taxes from corporate profits to pay back the government debt. The government then has to look to the smaller number of taxpayers for revenue and that means higher taxes.

How can the country hope to recover economically or create new jobs as long as money is leaving our country at these rates? This is exactly like people living on credit cards. Sooner or later, you have to pay the piper. The way to deal with that for a household is to cut the drain of money and/or find a way to make a lot more money. Fortunately, the U.S. is capable of making a lot more money. The sooner the country does that, as well as really focusing on stopping the money leaving our country, the better off the future will be.

Who thinks it might be a better idea to change the balance of trade to get out of trouble, rather than going deeper into debt? How can we change the balance of trade? How about we start with putting our biggest elephant on a diet and cut down Oil and Such by using domestically produced electricity instead.

It would be excellent if we could do this with domestically produced vehicles. The Cars and Parts elephant in this picture could also benefit from a going on a diet.

These numbers show there is a need for energy independence for very personal economic reasons. That is why energy independence is an issue that will appeal to and help unite people across all divides and persuasions. When you add the need for stable energy prices to the concern for our national security - and then throw in the impacts on our jobs and the economy, we come to a pretty clear Energy Secret.

Energy Secret
Energy independence is a key to the strength and future of ANY country.

The European Picture

If this is what happened in the U.S., then *what happened in the rest of the world to create the recession and lingering problems?*

A quick look at Europe shows that only four of the main economies produce any crude oil. Norway and Denmark are the only net exporters of oil in the bunch. The United Kingdom consumes just a bit more than it produces. Prior to 2005 England was a net exporter, coincidentally right before the recession. Italy consumes fourteen barrels of oil for each one it produces. It is close to being a total consumer.

The three substantial producers have recovered from the recession and experienced only minor problems, compared to most of the rest of the area.

All the rest of the countries are totally dependent on foreign oil to keep going. Some of these have large manufacturing bases that allow them to pay for the imported oil. The top of that list would be Germany and France. The countries without the oil or the manufacturing are the ones in the most trouble economically. The pundits are all looking at the E.U. government debt and the manufacturing but *how many are looking at the Oil and Such Elephant for the part it plays in the problem?*

Net oil-importing countries need better ideas and a new vision to get free from all the balance of trade concerns. Electric Vehicles are one piece of that puzzle that keeps your money in your country.

Creating Taxes

In a time of budget deficits and budget cuts, it becomes a real concern as to how we are going to provide the needed government services. Most people are either concerned about how to divide the existing pot of money the government has, how to do the budget cutting, or how to get more money in the pot through higher taxes. The issue of oil addiction puts another option on the table. It is the option of looking at where the money has gone that should be creating a healthy economy with more good jobs.

The balance of trade information above spells out clearly that large amounts of money are leaving our economy to pay for oil. It is like the pot of money the government is using has a huge leak in it. The leak is our tax base being exported as an integral part of our negative balance of trade.

This issue was highlighted at a California State Senate hearing for the Senate Transportation Committee. There were government agencies and elected officials making the case that spending for road repairs was a more pressing concern than spending on mass transit. It took a sustainable transport advocate to point out that encouraging driving cars was encouraging dollars to leave the country, which in turn means that the tax base is going with those dollars. Dollars spent on mass transit help stem that flow of dollars and keeps tax dollars refilling the pot.

This concern points to the need for mass transit for all socio economic levels, similar to those found in any well-developed metro area. It is also a consideration that applies to supporting the use of electric vehicles and others that run on domestically produced energy.

If any government wants the tax revenues to start flowing back into their budgets, they are going to have to do more to keep the tax base from leaking out of our country – along with our petro dollars.

Anyone can see this happening. It is in plain sight at every gas station in town. The next time you visit a station, try walking around the pumps to see how much people are spending on gasoline. Most people spend thirty dollars as a minimum and filling a twenty gallon tank can run over eighty dollars. Consider how many times this happens a day in your community, and you will quickly get a good idea of how many dollars are leaving your town by way of that gas station. In most places, the lion's share of that money ends up leaving the state. A recent study by the Union of Concerned Scientists called "Where Your Gas Money Goes" shows that ninety-eighty percent of the money spent on gasoline leaves a city. There is close to sixteen percent that pays taxes and expenses that benefit the state economy. The rest of the money (eighty-two percent) goes to oil companies, many of which are owned by OPEC countries and/or headquartered internationally. Nationally, somewhere up to half of the retail dollar has been leaving the country and that really adds up, as discussed in detail above.

What stores turn over the most dollars? Cities can figure this out by looking at their business license numbers. The short list would be gas stations, food stores, and big box stores. Both food stores and big box stores have similar local cash flows to gas stations. The big box stores are the ones who sell Chinese Consumer Goods. At least the U.S. is still producing most of its food, but the food production dollars still leave many communities and even most states. This adds up to these being not only the high dollar stores but they are the ones that result in the highest percentage of the dollars leaving the community. The owners and employees being the ones that get to keep the least amount per dollar spent.

Auto dealers will fit on that list in most cities as well. Their cash flow is similar to the other big chain companies (think Cars and Parts) with two exceptions. Typically auto retailers generate more sales tax and vehicle registration dollars for every dollar of revenue they generate. In addition, the domestic car companies support the largest remaining manufacturing base in the U.S., as would be the case in any car manufacturing country.

This relates to the idea of local living being part of building a sustainable economy. The more goods and services we can create locally for local consumption, the less transportation is needed and the more money stays in the local economy. Cutting the need for transportation by building up our local communities has huge potential to cut our oil imports. Farmers markets are great examples of things that help on this level. Promoting local business is another part of this, as is supporting and creating local culture with restaurants, entertainment and local arts.

The more people who drive EVs, the less money that will leave a local economy to pay for gasoline. That puts the people working at the local power company on the list of people who benefit from EVs. And they spend their paychecks in the local communities.

Fuel and the Housing Crisis

The main view of the 2008 economic crisis is that it started with the housing crisis. The housing crisis has been blamed in large part on the mortgage industry. But wait a minute... mortgage rates went down from about eight percent in 2000 to right at six percent in 2008 just before the housing collapse. Of course, some homeowners got in trouble with adjustable rate mortgages;

however, that would only be a problem for fancy mortgages that had a low starting rate that jumped up for some reason during this period. The straightforward fixed rate mortgages did not change. Standard adjustable rate mortgages actually would have followed the rates shown in the next graph and gone down in the period leading to the crash.

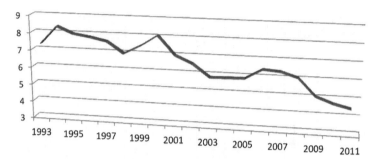

Mortgage Rates
30 Year Fixed Mortgage Rates by Percent
Data Source: U.S. Federal Reserve

The cost of houses went through the roof during the pre-crash period. Meanwhile, buyers thought they could pay for the more expensive prices at the low mortgage rates. *Was the whole problem due to people getting fancy deceptive mortgages or did something else happen to make it hard for people to pay their bills?*

The something else could well have been the cost of fuel. The graphs about personal energy security in Chapter 6 show what happened to fuel costs over the last two decades. In round numbers, the cost of gasoline went from about $1.50 per gallon in 2000 to $2.00 per gallon in 2004 and $4.00 in 2008 right before the housing collapse.

This idea that the fuel cost escalation was a significant part of creating the housing crisis leads to something else. It suggests that the fuel escalation actually led to the economic crisis or at least was a significant factor. *Does this make sense when we look at the numbers involved? Does it relate to where the housing crisis hit the hardest?*

People with long commutes are going to buy more gasoline than the average person with a short commute, all other things being equal. The more fuel they buy, the more they are hit by the price increases.

If we look at California, we can identify the places where people have the longest commutes. In the Los Angeles metro area, that would be the people in the Inland Empire, meaning Riverside and San Bernardino Counties. There are, or were, also people in Bakersfield and the High Desert with long commutes. In Northern California, those places include Stockton, Modesto, Salinas, Vacaville, and Fairfield - to name a few of the big ones.

Now, if you were to make a list of the places where the housing crisis hit the hardest and hit first, what would that list look like? For California, it would match very, very closely.

Is that a coincidence or is there a direct connection between people not having the money to pay their mortgage and the cost of fuel going up?

If we run some numbers on the people living in those areas you can see the impact of the fuel costs. A good mid-range start is with one person living in the Ontario area of the Inland Empire. It was and is common for people there to commute to Los Angeles for work. That commute can be 40 miles and more each way. This means that person would drive close to 1700 miles a month just to commute (21 days at 80 miles a day). Add a few miles for daily errands and for the weekend and we are pretty much looking to 1900 miles a month and more. In a vehicle that gets 20 miles per gallon, that would have cost about $140 per month in 2000. It would have cost $380 per month in 2008 in that same vehicle. That $240 per month increase would have happened quickly, with most of it happening between 2004 and 2008.

If that was happening to two people in that household then we are looking at an extra $500 per month after tax dollars leaving their household in just four years. That is a $6,000 increased expense per year (after tax) on median California household incomes of $57,000 (before tax) in 2008. That increase in cost is over ten percent of the median income before taxes!

If the household did not cut other expenses in that time, then **other** debt would start to happen pretty quickly. One way that debt was increasing was from home equity loans. The fast rise in housing prices created this option and there are reports that many people took on substantial amounts of this sort of debt. If the people and their neighbors increased their spending based on the increasing home equity, then the personal debt would have added up. With people paying that other debt, the mortgage *and* the increased fuel bill, you pretty much have a housing crisis on your hands.

These figures are for people with a 40 mile commute. There are longer commutes in these areas, given that going from San Bernardino to downtown L.A. is 60 miles each way. A drive from Stockton to Sacramento is 50 miles and from Stockton to Hayward is 60 miles. *Did you catch the part where Stockton is one of the first major California cities to seek bankruptcy protection?*

In addition, these figures are for people with a 20 MPG vehicle. Large SUVs and pickups are commonly used for commuting. They get 15 MPG on the highway. That would increase the added fuel cost to over $7,400 per year for two such vehicles on a 40 mile commute each way.

A ten percent increase in household expenses due to increased fuel cost could impact the viability of a house purchase. A family could have bought a new house in 2004 thinking they had the income to pay the extra expense. That income then went to pay for fuel and was not available to pay the mortgage. That starts to look like a causative influence on the housing crisis. If the housing crisis triggered the recession, we may have uncovered the deeper cause! It is almost certainly not the only cause, but it could be a significant part of the picture.

There are lots of people smarter than I am who can figure out if these details add up or not. With a little luck, they will get to that and soon. It could be important.

The importance of finding the real causes of a problem cannot be understated. It is only when the real causes are identified that the problem will find a lasting solution.

It is also important that we take the change in our balance of trade seriously. We need to know the extent to which this is the underlying cause of our economic problems. Only then can we take the appropriate actions.

In the meantime, all the uncertainties that go along with any and all of the concerns tied to oil are impacting our lives. Perhaps there are steps we can each take to provide a little more certainty and security at a personal level. There is more on this in the next chapter.

Links on the Economy

Balance of Trade Data
www.census.gov/foreign-trade/Press-Release/current_press_release/
www.census.gov/foreign-trade/statistics/historical/gands.txt
www.bea.gov/international/index.htm#bop
http://tse.export.gov/TSE/TSEHome.aspx
http://tse.export.gov/TSE/TSEOptions.aspx

GDP and Personal Income:
www.census.gov/hhes/www/income/data/statemedian/
www.bea.gov/national/

National Debt
www.treasurydirect.gov/govt/reports/pd/mspd/2012/2012_dec.htm
www.treasurydirect.gov/govt/reports/pd/mspd/2011/2011_dec.htm
www.treasurydirect.gov/govt/reports/pd/histdebt/histdebt_histo5.htm

Interest Rates
www.federalreserve.gov/releases/H15/data.htm

Money Supply
www.federalreserve.gov/datadownload/

Union of Concerned Scientists
Where Your Gas Money Goes
www.ucsusa.org/gasmoney

Chapter 6

Personal Energy Security

There is good news about finding a way to help with the all the oil-related issues. Here it is… The solutions can help us with our personal energy security.

The most personal part of our oil habit is how much money is leaving our lives to pay for it. There are very few who have not felt the pinch from the price at the pump in recent years. It is one thing to have to hand over a good chunk of money on a regular basis and another to see the wild swings in gas prices.

It is pretty clear that we have two things going on all the time. One is a steady increase in the price of gasoline. The other thing is the wild ups and downs in the price. Price gyrations happen every time some sort of real glitch occurs in the supply or some other event lets the oil speculators destabilize the price.

The steady price increase is a global market issue. The increasing population needs more oil and the supply is having trouble keeping up. Add to that the issue that people in the U.S.A. use several times more oil than anyone else on the planet and it gets more challenging. Given that the rest of the world would like to use as much as the U.S., there is a lot of long-term pressure on the price of oil.

The wild swings in price are usually tied to international events. A revolution here, a war there, a ship blown up or some serious act of terrorism and the price of gasoline takes off. A small drop in the supply combined with the consistent demand means the price is going to jump up.

There is another international trend that seems to be happening. It is a cycle of increased demand as the economy gets better and a drop in demand if the economy slows down. If the oil supply stays steady, then the price goes up as people and businesses get more active. The more people commuting and driving as part of their work, the higher the demand and the prices go up. The biggest example of this was the increase in price through 2007, followed by the drop in price after the 2008 economic crisis. The market seems like it has been doing this on a smaller scale ever since.

If all of these sorts of things happen at once - then watch out!

The price of energy going up is not a problem if your income is going up with it. As that has not been the case for the majority of people in recent years, then the problem becomes personal.

How will you be able to afford the energy to do what you need to do if this continues?

That is the issue of personal energy security.

Domestic Energy

One thing that might help would be to only use fuel produced in this country. That would reduce the impact of international events on our supply. It would not solve the entire international market concern because the price of domestic supplies is influenced significantly by the international prices. But it could help with stability and it would help our economy.

The reality is that over sixty percent of the crude oil used in this country comes from overseas. This means there are two choices for getting away from that. One is to cut our consumption by sixty percent. The other is to more than double the production or perhaps some of both.

Doubling the production is a nice idea on a couple of levels. It sounds like a good simple fix, so why not give it a try? It appeals to people who seem to have a limited knowledge of these complex issues and who are primarily clear about what they want.

The trouble is that the reverse has been happening. The U.S. oil production has been declining since the 1970s with some increases since 2005. That was the case because imported oil became much less expensive. In addition, the oil in this country became more expensive to produce. Production has gone up but only since the price went up and even then not to the previous levels up until now.

Another part this is - *How smart is it to use up all the oil as fast as possible?* The new technology or unconventional extraction techniques has made it possible to get every last drop of available oil out of the known reserves. That oil will be needed to run the country a hundred years from now as well. *Is the current generation so special that it deserves to use up all our natural resource just because we want the oil?* If we were really special, we would be good stewards who allocate those resources wisely with a long-term view.

Besides, *who among us really has any control over how much oil is produced?* What we do have control over is how much we each actually use.

Electricity and Gas Prices

There are very few sources of energy that are real alternatives to using fossil fuel oil. This is particularly true for personal transportation. If we are to consider using electric vehicles, it would be important that they provide a real benefit.

The price we pay for electricity has a very different pricing system than oil has. It is based in part on the availability of natural gas and of coal for much of the world. Both of these are available in large quantities domestically. The other energy sources include things like wind, hydro and solar, which are cleaner and renewable sources. Some cultures rely on oil. There is also the ugly step-child - which would be the nuclear power that has all sorts of issues tied to it.

One thing shared by most of these is that they are predominantly domestic sources - that are tied to creating jobs and building our national economy. When domestic sources of energy add to our national security, this in turn adds to your personal energy security.

Another thing that's different about electrical rates is they are regulated under most circumstances. For better or worse, there are government agencies that have a say in the prices utilities can charge for a kilowatt hour (kWh). The very least that comes from this is that the rates change more slowly and they are not able to jump up and down the way gasoline prices do. That adds another element of personal energy security.

The big issue is what will happen to the price of electricity over the long term. One answer comes from looking at the historic trends, as the following table shows.

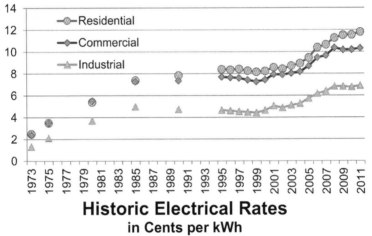

Historic Electrical Rates
in Cents per kWh
Data Source: U.S. Energy Information Administration (E.I.A).
Monthly Energy Review September 2012

There is clearly a long-term price increase. It is steady and reasonable, given that it went from under 8 cents a kWh in 1990 to 12 cents in 2012. That is a fifty percent increase over twenty-two years, which works out to just over two percent a year. That is below general inflation.

The commercial and industrial rates shown indicate a good advantage for fleets that can access those pricing structures.

The increase in the price per kWh shows a sharp contrast to the increase in gasoline prices. The next graph presents the historic gasoline prices.

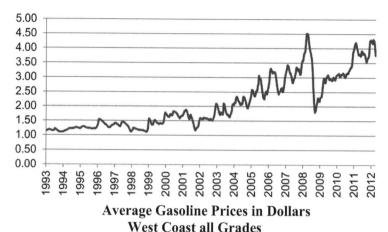

Average Gasoline Prices in Dollars
West Coast all Grades
Data Source: U.S. Energy Information Administration (E.I.A)

The cost of gasoline went up by **ONE HUNDRED AND EIGHTY-TWO** percent in the period from 1990 to 2012. That works out to be close to **EIGHT** percent a year, and it has been almost four times as fast as the cost of electricity. It is higher than the rate of general inflation. This strongly suggests that gasoline prices are one of the big factors in driving inflation.

COMPARISON OF PRICE INCREASES

		1990	2012	Percent Increase	Percent Per year
Gasoline, Regular	per gallon	$ 1.30	$ 3.66	182%	8%
Electricity, Residential	per kW	$ 0.08	$ 0.12	50%	2%

This is a pretty good indication of where your path to personal energy security could be.

It would be helpful to be able to directly compare the energy pricing from the two graphs above even though the two energy sources have a different pricing unit. We can do that by equating a specific amount of electricity to a gallon of gas that is equivalent. The government specifications for a *gallon of gasoline equivalent (GGE)* uses 33.7 kW hours to compare the two, as will be discussed in more detail when we get to the specifics about EVs and Mileage Ratings. The next graph uses this conversion factor to show the relative cost of electricity and gasoline since 1995.

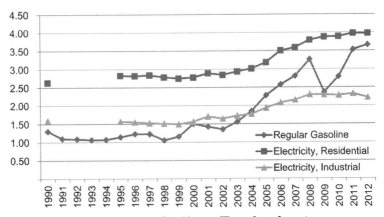

Cost per Gallon Equivalent
(in Dollars)

The historic trends in this graph show the gradual rise in industrial and commercial prices for electricity. The erratic and fast rise of the gasoline prices shows the uncertainty and expense of the fuel. Which lines indicate a clear direction that will provide more personal energy security? If history was the only factor, the choice would be simple. There is more to it than that.

One thing that is very interesting to see is that the cost of the energy in electricity has only recently come on par with the energy cost of gasoline. Clearly industrial electrical costs are lower than the same energy costs in gasoline and residential costs are also getting closer. The commercial rates (not shown on the graph) were lower for electricity starting in 2011.

Energy Secret
Industrial users have only just recently started to pay less for the energy in electricity than they pay for the energy in a gallon of gasoline. Consumers are getting very close.

That is a historic turn of events.

EVs typically travel three times as far as a gas car on the same amount of energy. This higher energy efficiency makes for a significant advantage. When the cost for the energy in electricity is the same as it is in gasoline, then the advantage of the three-fold energy efficiency is fully realized.

Which direction does this price convergence suggest for your personal energy security?

Future Cost Factors

Another concern about the cost of electricity is if something will cause the cost to go up more rapidly. *Is there some part of the electrical generation system what will be hit by substantial price increases?*

Nuclear energy is the part of the generation system that has shown signs of being most susceptible to a cost increase. The tsunami disaster in Japan has pointed to both a large risk factor with a huge cost of cleanup. There is also a need to provide better and costly protection for future power plants. The closure at the San Onofre power plant points to a shorter life span and higher end of life costs that will need to be paid somehow. Then there is a persistent concern about storage of the spent fuel. This has yet to be resolved with a permanent solution as the costs have been unacceptable.

Coal costs could stay close to the same for many years, at least on the energy supply side. The statistics show over a hundred year supply on hand. This would translate into added stability in electrical costs, all other things being equal. Coal is also embroiled in a whole range of issues and what it will cost to handle all of them. Alternatively, how much will it cost if we do NOT handle the concerns being raised about coal, all of which are beyond the scope of this book.

One of the most stable cost situations is for using natural gas for electrical generation. The advent of horizontal drilling combined with hydraulic fracturing or fracking has lowered the fuel cost. That combination presents the promise of massive and cheap supplies for over a hundred years. The ancillary issues are less than with coal but are still a concern. Plus the fracking technology may be adjusted and become more expensive to handle the various water quality and earth stability concerns that are coming to light.

Bio gas from landfills and from agricultural waste is very close to the cost of natural gas from drilling. Technology improvements may close that gap and will help to keep the price of mined natural gas in check. The other advantage to bio gas is that it can be created almost anywhere and can become a locally supplied transportation fuel.

Good news also applies to renewable sources such as solar and wind. The cost of both of these is coming down and becoming more competitive with traditional sources. The developments in residential solar systems are actually remarkable in nature and scope. The system costs have come down substantially - on the order of a one-third reduction since 2008. The regulatory changes in many places including California are increasing the value of the solar power generated. These increases are based on the solar electric system generating during peak demand times. These and other changes are radically reducing the time it takes for a solar system to pay for itself. That is so much the case that this is one of the major themes for *Energy and EVs Book Two.*

Some of these various energy sources come with related potential cost increases. All of this is relatively minor compared with the accelerating cost of our dependence on foreign oil.

As mentioned, an optimistic report on the energy future is the *World Energy Outlook Report 2012.* It reports a well-documented projection for electricity costs in the U.S. for the year 2035. That projection is for approximately 14 cents per kWh. That is up from the current average of 12 cents per kWh. That is probably adjusted for inflation and is less than a twenty percent increase in over twenty years.

If we are to use electricity for our transportation needs, we will need more than just a reliable and affordable fuel source. We will need affordable electric vehicles and e-bikes that fit our needs. That is why *Energy and EV Savings*, the second book in this series, addresses exactly how EVs can fit into your life. That book's working subtitle gives a good idea about what is covered: *How to use the Volt, electric cars, plug-in hybrids and e-bikes to cut your gas cost and get close to zero fuel cost with solar electricity.*

One of the important considerations for all the cost increases tied to electrical generation is the domestic supply part of this. Any cost tied to the domestic production of electricity is money being spent within our country. That money is going to create jobs and business for national interests. It stays in our economy and gives us the money we need to pay for our energy needs. In contrast, money spent on gasoline leaves the country at a rate of close to 50 cents on the dollar.

So which energy source points to a personal energy secure future, oil or electricity?

Links on Personal Security

Oil Costs
www.shalebubble.org
www.fuelgaugereport.aaa.com
www.iea.org/stats/index.asp

Center for Transportation Research,
Argonne National Laboratory
www.transportation.anl.gov/pdfs/TA/635.PDF
http://greet.es.anl.gov

Chapter 7

The EV Solution

This is all very big stuff. The good part is that you can help with all this.

What can you as one person or one household do to help with these problems?

There is a simple answer. This is a really big Energy Secret.

Energy Secret
In order to help stop the energy-related concerns -
STOP being part of the problem.

So what does it take to stop being part of the oil dependence problem? A minimum in the U.S. would be cutting your oil consumption by more than half. With more than forty percent of our oil needs coming from imported sources, cutting your consumption for all travel in half would reduce your use by about that amount. It would even free up some domestically produced oil to cover the production and transportation of the food and consumer goods you buy.

These problems are huge because they are the accumulation of the impact of 350 million problems, at least here in the U.S. That is approximately how many people we have in this country, in case you are wondering where that number came from. You can opt out of being part of this by figuring out how to live without using oil for transportation.

The *EV SOLUTION* is a way to do this right now and with the least amount of change of any other option available. It is not the only solution we will need over the next thirty years, as transportation is a very complex issue. The EV solution is one part of the solution and it is the easiest and the most fun way to go for personal transportation. The rest of this book will show you how that works and what is involved with you becoming part of this solution.

The even better news about doing this is that it works for you as well. When you stop using oil, the gas-related security issues stop impacting your life. You are no longer subject to the tyranny of the price at the pump. Increasingly large sums of money stop flowing out of your life and you gain a stronger sense of personal energy security.

Getting to that minimum reduction is not very hard at this point. It could be as simple as riding your bicycle or e-bike for all your trips around town. It happens the minute you buy an all-electric vehicle (AEV) or a plug-in hybrid EV (PHEV) like a Volt.

There is another step you can take after getting a clear idea about the EV solution that this book intends to provide for you. That step is to look at the nuts and bolts of how the EV solution would actually work for your personal situation. This means seeing how an EV would handle your transportation needs and how you would get the electricity you need to get to where you want to go. *Energy and EV Savings*, the second book in this series, will go step-by-step through all the details about how to use an EV effectively and drive on nearly free fuel from the sun.

Freedom from Imported Oil

Anyone driving a pure electric vehicle has taken a step out of this cycle. Their bank accounts are no longer controlled by the events that impact the price at the pump. Instead they are paying the more stable prices of domestically produced electricity.

There are a lot of EV owners who have taken a next step, which is to produce the electricity they use for themselves. With a little extra capacity on a photovoltaic (PVC) solar electric system, they are driving on sunshine.

So how does oil independence work with a car like the Chevy Volt? The Volt is an awesome, hot and affordable car that can be your personal solution. Here is how that works.

Let's say you are driving a reasonably fuel-efficient vehicle already. An example would be a Chevy Cruz, which gets 33.3 MPG and has a similar size and capacity to the Volt. If everyone was driving something with that mileage, our oil imports would drop substantially. That is better mileage than many vehicles, given the national average is close to 26 MPG for cars. A Cruze would use about 12 gallons to go 400 miles.

It is fairly easy for the Chevy Volt people to use 3 gallons of gas to go 400 miles. That is what happened as soon as I started driving my Volt. That is for normal driving while charging at home. That nets out to 135 MPG for the gasoline used. It is a reduction of seventy-five percent in oil usage. That Chevy Volt can easily claim to be off the imported oil habit. If everyone did that, we would be done with imported oil and moving toward more personal energy security.

EV Smile
Realizing you just bought a car that means you no longer need to send money to OPEC every week.

Since I first started using my Volt, I have been able to go 1700 miles using only 3 gallons of gas. Some people do even better.

All of this also means a reduction in the money going from your personal bank accounts to pay for fuel.

A Perfect Day with a Chevy Volt

Those of you who are wondering just what it is like to get these sorts of results might benefit from reading about one of my early driving experiences. A 120-plus-mile round-trip drive from Ventura to Santa Monica was a great example of what to expect when you first start driving a vehicle like the Volt. That trip has become smoother and easier since this first try but see if you can find the hard part.

I started my day with a full charge on my battery. That let me pick my friend up at her home in Ventura and start the drive through Malibu. We enjoyed the sun, the ocean, the view of the islands and dodged many bicycles as we cruised the coast. The generator started up and we did not even notice it.

When I began the drive, my trip meter was showing an average of around 103 MPG. By the time we got to the Rose Cafe in Venice, it was right at 100 MPG.

After a nice lunch with friends, we looked for a charge station at a couple of locations near our next destination in Mar Vista. The nearest one was farther than we thought from the location of the Tango studio we were visiting. It did not work to charge the car during that part of the visit. The good thing about the Volt is that it did not matter.

We enjoyed our Tango afternoon and then headed towards the Electric Lodge back in Venice. The five Blink chargers in the parking lot were not fully functional yet so we could not use them. That discouraged a walk on Abbot Kinney or a coffee at Abbots Habit, both old favorite pastimes in that charming shopping and restaurant district. In addition, the charging stations required a magic card that I did not have. I have since been able to get one of those from the Blink website, so that is now handled.

Special thanks to Joel at the Electric Lodge for getting those chargers. He is definitely one of the good guys.

Our next stop was to go to Santa Monica's Third Street Promenade and drive by the new bicycle center. That center has rentals, bike storage, lockers and a shower. It is such a cool place and one of the results created by people in the Sustainable Transport Club (STC). Plus, it's right near the electric chargers in the parking garage. Those are another STC-supported result.

Now one of these six charging stations is a Clipper Creek. It's easy and free to use, which is why a Nissan LEAF was using it. The other chargers were all Charge Point units, which were a little more challenging.

The charger says to place your key here, in front of the main display. Well it turns out that it does not mean your car key. It also turns out that the lack of a MasterCard or other credit card symbol was an indication that these meters were actually free. Five minutes later, my phone call resulted in my vehicle being charged and a promise of special pay-pass key being in the mail. That key would put me on my way to using all Charge-Point machines easily and quickly, starting immediately with the free ones. It is best to go online and handle your request in detail. The phone call did not get results on the card.

After a pleasant visit with friends and a little shopping, the Volt had 12 miles of battery charge.

We started back home with a nice drive through Malibu. It was dinnertime when we got to the charging station by Malibu City Hall. The Volt generator had just barely kicked in before we plugged into the charging station. A relaxed meal at the Marmalade Cafe and a leisurely stroll back to the car and we had another 19 miles of charge. Once again, it's free!

By the time we finished the 120 mile round-trip, my trip meter was still over 100 miles per gallon but we had used less than 2 gallons of gas for the day. My previous car would have used about 5 gallons for that trip. That means I have cut my fuel use by 60 percent. And that is for a long trip. That meant I was virtually free from imported oil.

Given that my local area trips are at least *NINETY PERCENT* oil-free, the solution is really working.

Since this early experience, that same trip is now being done with only using one gallon of gas. The difference is in both my planning and better charging setups. There are better charging options now and they improve steadily. This includes more chargers and the fact that both my Charge Point and Blink cards are in my wallet and fully operational.

The maps for finding the charging stations are also improving steadily. The links at the end of this chapter will take you to the mapping websites, some of which have mobile apps. That list also includes the websites to get the activation cards you might need in your area.

One trick that is working is to plan enough time to charge in Malibu on the way into Santa Monica. There are three chargers there and they are all free. I allow an extra hour on the trip. That gives me time to get the charge I need to get into Santa Monica on all electric.

It is not hard to make the most of that charge time. One option is a good brisk walk through the lovely area. My second choice is an hour spent at a coffee shop with a little WI-FI or some laptop word processing. OK, sometimes it is just a coffee and newspaper break or perhaps lunch. Any time spent hanging in a beautiful place like Malibu is time well spent.

Another planning difference is that it is easier to get a full charge while in Santa Monica. It is reasonably easy to end my stay with a full 35 to 40 mile charge. The charging for the trip includes a full charge to start the day, a full charge before heading home and another ten miles of charge on route. That adds up so there is less than 40 miles to drive on gasoline, which means less than one gallon of gas. Life is good and imported oil free!

Taking that trip in an 80-mile range, battery-only vehicle - an AEV 80 - could have been done. It would have required better planning. It might have required more time near the charger. A trip to Long Beach would only have been convenient in the Volt. Clearly, any two-car household needs one of each. *Which of these vehicles is your next step?*

EV Smiles

There are lots of reasons for buying an EV, including the motivations that put an EV smile on your face. An EV smile is a phenomenon tied to how great these vehicles are to drive and how much fun they can be.

This is where we get to stop being so serious and get to the good part. That means we get to lighten up and look at the possibilities - instead of all the problems. You will see more EV smiles called out like the one below.

The EV smile phenomenon was first identified by people giving test-rides to people new to EVs. It seemed that the new drivers were almost universally ending up with this serene and slightly naughty smile by the end of the ride. It is a very specific look.

The EV veterans who were giving these test-rides would nod when they noticed the smile and remember their "first-time feeling." The veterans then compared notes and found out it happened with all sorts of EVs. It happens with electric bicycles, electric motor scooters and electric motorcycles (actually the e-motorcycles tend to result in really big grins). It happens with electric cars and plug-in hybrids. Heck, it happens when just riding in the Tesla Roadster, let alone driving it.

EV Smile
Happens with the first test-drive you take in an EV.
Warning: This smile may repeat numerous times with every new
type of EV you try.

One thing that can get an EV smile is that some EVs look so hot that they are collectible items. The whole Tesla line falls into that category as did the Fisker. Both of these have been repeatedly shown to be so exciting that they fall well into the hot and sexy car category; so much so that there is a whole discussion about sexy cars below.

How EVs Fit

Here is a quick overview of what we are dealing with. Some of this may not make sense now, but it will by the time you finish this book.

Electric vehicles have more range than most people drive in their normal daily living. If you drive within the range of your EV almost all the time then life is good. This means driving locally in your all-electric vehicle.

When people drive longer distances, it means they have to charge their batteries on the road. If there are chargers that let that work easily, then life is still good and you are still in an *All-Electric Vehicle (AEV)*. If the chargers are not so available or take too much time, then you might be a candidate for a *Plug-in Hybrid EV (PHEV)*. The more you drive to places out of your local area, the less likely you are to use an AEV or you would need a more expensive AEV.

The bigger the vehicle, the more expensive it is to get long range on an AEV. You can drive big AEVs locally. If you need to drive big vehicles all the time, it is less likely it will be an AEV and more likely it would be a PHEV. You can drive big PHEVs anywhere and they are coming soon.

People who drive really long distances with stop-and-go traffic may benefit from a standard hybrid vehicle. If the long distances are driven at highway or freeway speeds all the time, then the hybrid will not do you much good.

People who drive really big vehicles very long distances probably will not benefit from a hybrid or any kind of EV.

How do you figure out where the lines are on all of these general ideas? There are two things you can do to get clear about this. One is to get a better understanding of the vehicles from this book. The other thing is to sort through your habits and look at the facts about your situation and needs. It takes crunching some numbers and taking a hard look at the places you live and drive. *Energy and EV Savings*, the second book in this series, will step you through how to get your facts straight and seeing just how the facts relate to using an EV.

There is more to the decision than just the facts, though. For one thing, most of these electric vehicles are awesome to drive. The manufacturers are adding some really great features that create lots of added value. They are quiet, smooth, have great torque and handle like sports cars. The original Tesla Sports model is so fast and handles so well that it is in the same class as any fine sports car like the Lotus. The Volt takes a mountain road as well as almost any car made in America. It is not as quick as a Corvette, but it is smoother.

EVs come in all sorts of shapes and sizes with different capabilities. This book will include a look at the features and specifications both for All-Electric Vehicles (AEVs) and for Plug-in Hybrid EVs (PHEVs). It will also cover some other types of EVs, including the most-affordable ones like the *e-bikes* and *Neighborhood Electric Vehicles (NEVs)*. That way you can buy the right vehicle for your needs.

The hardest part of all this is that we have to make changes in what we do and how we think about our lives.

EVs Mean Change

Have you ever noticed that there are a lot of people who resist change? Like almost everyone you know! There is value in that, as it helps provide stability and consistency in our lives. When people are in that mode, we hold on to the way we have been thinking about things as long as we can.

It is unfortunate that energy challenges mean confronting change. The older I get, the more I resist change. For instance, it took five women ganging up on me to get me to use a cell phone. One of them was a truly beautiful red-headed tango-dancing ballerina. You can let your imagination run wild about the other four.

Now I am dragging my feet about going to a smart phone. Both of my sisters are using them and most of my friends. I really do not want to go through figuring out which one is right for me. I do not want to change the way I use my phone again. That is a little like how my mother was with her cell phone. (Oops - two sisters and a mother, *am I blowing your illusions about the other four women?* Only one more to go...)

The fact that you have read this far does mean something. It means that you will be able to make the transition a little more easily than most people. My block with the smart phone has to do with sorting through all the technology and options and figuring out what I need. This book will get you through that with the EVs and hopefully include a little fun along the way.

A New Way of Thinking

There are some very basic differences between the gas and electric drive technologies. This calls for a new way of thinking to sort out your specific driving needs. This new way of thinking is called *the EV mindset*. It is the EV mindset that lets people get into using an EV. Holding onto gasoline-centric thinking is what is keeping many people from making the change. For lots of those people, understanding the EV mindset is the only thing that needs to change for an EV to work for them. This book will give you a clear look at the EV mindset so you can decide if it works for you.

There are some people who have already changed their thinking about transportation. They figured out that an electric vehicle will work for them. They were able to do that because they started to think like an EV driver. They entered into the EV mindset.

That is a little like entering the Twilight Zone, but even more like entering into the future of energy-efficient transportation. It is sort of like exploring the new frontier and going where no man has gone before. That is, except it is very "down to earth." The EV mindset involves practicalities that help solve real-world problems.

People who do NOT own EVs think about cars with a gasoline-centric thinking. That mindset has become entrenched and is based on using an Internal Combustion Engine (an ICE). EV drivers call that ICE thinking.

ICE thinking creates one or more reasons that an EV will not work for the person. Some people think it is the cost of the vehicles. Some people think it is the charging infrastructure. Some people think it is the range of the batteries. These may all play a role but what if the big deal was -

HOW people think about EVs?

ICE thinking finds one EV specification that does not fit their idea of a good vehicle. The mindset uses that specification to stay with their ICE until an EV becomes an ICE vehicle. Perhaps that person does not care that the fuel cost is sucking large amounts of money out of their lives and out of the economy. ICE thinking wants to believe that we will find a way to solve all the problems tied to ICE vehicles without noticing the change.

The big question for most people is about the cost. Stories of $100,000 EVs will raise that sort of issue.

Many people do not understand how affordable these vehicles can be. They see the sticker price and walk away. Several less obvious things impact the cost of the vehicle. Not the least of these is the *incentives* provided by local, state and federal government programs. A close look at all the savings can help you get clear about how to make EVs work for you.

The good news about all this is that it can be fun to see transportation from the new perspective. The many ways an EV mindset can give a fun new perspective will be explored throughout the rest of this book.

Links on the EV Solution

Charger Maps
www.afdc.energy.gov/afdc/locator/stations/
http://electric.carstations.com
www.evchargermaps.com
www.evchargernews.com
http://openchargemap.sourceforge.net
www.plugshare.com
www.recargo.com
www.teslamotors.com/supercharger

Charging Networks
Charge Point America – Coulomb Technologies
www.chargepointamerica.com
www.mychargepoint.net

ECOtality - Blink
www.ecotality.com
www.blinknetwork.com

NRG Energy, eVgo network system
www.evgonetwork.com

350 Green Network
www.350green.com

Others
www.shorepower.com
www.semacharge.com
www.carcharging.com

Chapter 8

Costs and EV Savings

The idea that the cost of an EV is a significant barrier to using an EV creates a strong contrast between ICE thinking and the EV mindset. Here is a secret that comes from the EV mindset.

EV Secret
EVs are the cheapest vehicles to drive on the road.

ICE thinking will respond along the lines of: Wait just a minute. *How can a $110,000 car be the cheapest? That is a really expensive car.*

OK, I'm messing with you here more than just a little, ***or am I?!***

There are a lot of people who look at the $40k MSRP on the Volt or the $29k MSRP on the LEAF and walk away thinking they are too expensive. That is the ICE mindset getting to them. The actual cost of driving an EV can be really low - once you get over the hurdle of buying one.

Most of the time, electric vehicles cost as little as 3 cents a mile to drive. This is based on the fuel use reported by the Environmental Protection Agency (EPA) when electricity costs 12 cents per kWh. A $90,000 Tesla Model S might cost as much as 5 cents a mile in energy costs to drive.

But wait; then there are the cars on *solar photovoltaic systems* that are using free energy. OK, maybe not totally free, but real close to it. The chapter on *Driving on Sunshine* in *Energy and EV Savings* will describe that in detail.

A passenger car that gets 30 MPG will cost over 13 cents a mile in gasoline at $4.00 per gallon. That is four times as expensive as an EV.

Costs and the EV Mindset

The EV mindset says that paying $50 per month for domestically produced fuel is a lot cheaper than paying $250 a month for oil-based fuel. The EV mindset also sees that having a photovoltaic system on your roof means that $50 goes toward paying for something you own and adds value to your property.

ICE thinking considers buying an economy car for $15K a good deal - *without* thinking about the $25,000 it will cost for oil-based fuel over ten years.

The EV mindset looks at the lifetime use of the vehicle and compares the cost of the vehicle, plus the fuel. From that point of view, you can see that you could buy an EV for $35K and pay $5,000 for fuel over ten years. That EV would be a pretty nice car that is quiet and considerably better than an entry level economy car.

Both cars cost the same over the ten years, but one is a nicer car and does not come with all the problems of oil addiction.

The lifetime cost for your vehicle will depend on how you drive, etc. It is also impacted by tax credits, which can cut your costs by up to $9,000.

There is a rich dad, poor dad thing going on with these two ways of thinking. The road to the results that a rich dad would travel is the one with the EV. This is not just because a rich dad has the money. It is because this is how wealthy people think about things. They know a good investment when they see one. They would buy the EV within their corporations and get the depreciation credit from the investment. That is why they have the money to buy an EV.

Clearly, there is a need to sort all of these details out. There are a lot of people who think that EVs are just too expensive. The people who buy them know they are cheap to keep, so how does all of that work out?

There are sections in this book that will go into all of these concerns in detail. The following simple example will give you a taste of how that can work and points to a way to get started that does not require much cash up front.

Lease a LEAF
A good example of cost savings is leasing a LEAF. You can lease a base LEAF for less than $200 per month. It is a fantastic car with loads of extra features. That lease price is so low because there is tax incentives involved as discussed in the Tax Advantages part of this book. These tax incentives put all the normal concerns about leasing a car out the window as they reduce the vehicle cost by $7,500.

The fuel costs for a LEAF are rated at $1.02 for 25 miles by the EPA. The lease allows 12K miles a year (close to the national average) before extra fees kick in. The EPA cost works out to about $40 per month if you drive all 12K miles over the year. Comparable fuel costs on a reasonably priced compact car that gets 25 MPG average would be $160 per month at $4.00 per gallon. These comparable fuel costs mean a total EV savings of $120 per month or more (given that the maintenance costs will also be less on an EV). If you subtract the $120 EV savings from the lease, then your EV lease would compare to an $80 lease on an ICE vehicle. *What kind of new car can you lease or own in any way for $80 a month?* It would be very pale compared to the LEAF.

It can be even better than this example shows. There is one LEAF driver who gets free charging at work and has a free charger in his neighborhood at home. That means really close to zero fuel costs for this guy with his LEAF! He was paying $300 a month for just his fuel. He is driving a new car and paying less per month than he was for just his former fuel cost!

That may not last forever, but it will be fun in the meantime. *Did I mention that this driver had a really wide smile as he told the story?*

But wait; there is more (as they say in the TV ads for mattresses). The lease has a $1,800 down payment. The person taking that lease in California is probably eligible to get a check from the state for $2,500, so there is no net out of pocket cost, and you will put money in the bank! *Are you starting to see why so many well-educated people are getting these vehicles?*

EV Smile
Telling how the state gave you $700 dollars to get a brand-new vehicle you can charge for free at home and at work.

Is Price Really the Issue?

The ICE mindset will let people buy cars that are a lot more expensive than most EVs. If the cost of the vehicle was the thing that kept them off the road, there would be no luxury cars. There are many cars on the road that cost more than the current EVs.

Is the cost of a Mercedes keeping those cars from showing up on the roads? There are lots of people who can afford a Mercedes, or a Porsche, or a Land Rover or any of a long list of vehicles that cost over $40k. When all of these own an EV, then the cost issue might be the limiting factor. Until that is the case, then it is the perception of the cost that is the issue. That perception is part of ICE thinking.

Any expensive vehicle is being used because the person who bought it thinks it has a value equal to or better than the price. Expensive vehicles have a quiet ride, luxury, safety, lots of features and prestige. Prestige can be one of the biggest parts of this and it is usually based on the price of the vehicle.

An EV mindset says that the best feature to have is one that does not feed our oil addiction. That would be an electric drive. The EV mindset says that prestige comes with helping to solve our pressing problems, including national security and stopping the drain of oil dollars leaving our economy.

Part of prestige is the respect you give a person. *Who would you respect more, someone driving an Audi R8 getting 11 miles per gallon or someone driving a Tesla Roadster and setting the pace for an oil-free lifestyle?* FYI: they both go zero to 60 mph in 3.7 seconds but the Audi costs more.

The point that the price is not the issue came up during a recent visit with fellow EV advocate Kelly Olsen. He has taken to counting how many EVs he sees when out and about in L.A. The visit involved tea, coffee and pastry at a lovely cafe overlooking San Vicente at the border between Santa Monica and Brentwood. That is the Brentwood of OJ infamy.

This occurred recently just after Tesla reported selling more vehicles in the first quarter of 2013 than any other EV model. The Tesla vehicles sold up to that time all went for over $80k, compared to the Volts at $40k and LEAFs priced at $32k. By the time Kelly and I had counted up to nineteen EVs, we had gone from amused, to shocked, to being in awe. Of the nineteen EVs that drove past, twelve of them were a Tesla, five were Volts and only two were LEAFs! Evidently people in that area were clear that price was not the concern. They just wanted to drive awesome vehicles with high prestige and status.

As we walked back to my humble Volt, we ran across one more Tesla and succumbed to an EV Smile.

EV Smile
The twentieth EV spotted in less than an hour and a half was another Tesla. Clearly, price was not the issue.

It was a gorgeous Tesla with the high performance package which would have been well over $100k. The smile repeated with the next four or five EVs that showed up on my drive home.

Unfortunately, one reason other people are not getting a full-speed EV is that they do not have money in the bank to buy one outright. The EV mindset knows that one reason people do not have the money is because they spend so much paying for fuel. If we could just cut our fuel costs, we would be able to pay for the EV.

Fortunately there are ways to cut that fuel costs including leasing an EV, which can be particularly advantageous as we just discovered. Other ways include using Neighbor Electric

Vehicles (NEVs), e-motorcycles and e-bicycles around your local area. These can cut your fuel costs in half and let you save the difference toward a full-size EV. They also take the burden off your current vehicle so they will last a few years longer and give you the time to save up for the bigger EVs.

This is one element of EV magic. Electric vehicles keep money in your life and in your country. You have already looked at how important that can be.

There is a whole chapter on *The EV Mindset* - Chapter 10. In that, you can read about things other than cost that impact your options. These include ideas like understanding the benefits of having a full tank of electricity every morning and managing your family fleet. There will be other EV mindset ideas that come up throughout this book.

It Comes Down to Efficiency

What is it that makes EVs stand out from other types of vehicles? Could it be the efficiency? Electric drives use a really high percentage of the energy put into them for the purposes of getting down the road. That means they are "energy efficient." The efficiency lets them operate with really low fuel costs. The mileage these vehicles get shows how that efficiency works. The Volt allows a good evaluation of this. It can run on batteries. It can also run on the gasoline-burning generator. It is sufficiently similar to the Chevy Cruze that the mileage of the Cruze running a gas engine is a reasonable comparison. Here are the EPA combined miles per gallon ratings for driving both highway and city for each option:

ENERGY EFFICIENCY COMPARISON

Vehicle	Driving Mode	Combined MPG - EPA
Chevy Cruze	Running on gas engine	30 MPG
Chevy Volt	Running on gas generator	40 MPG
Chevy Volt	Running on battery electric	94 MPGe*

*MPGe stands for MPG equivalent, see Chapter 12, *Basic EV Considerations*

The Volt, which is heavier than the Cruze, gets better mileage - even when burning gas for the generator. Why?... Because it is *more efficient*.

The Volt gets even better mileage when running on battery power. That is by more than twice the mileage the Volt gets using the gasoline generator. It gets more than three times the mileage on battery electric than the Cruze on gasoline. Why?... Because it is more efficient.

The general rule of thumb is that an electric vehicle is three times more energy efficient than a vehicle powered by an internal combustion engine (ICE) using gasoline only. The low energy efficiency is due to the ICE losing a lot of energy to heat. The electric vehicle loses less heat and also gains efficiency by getting energy back when it slows down or goes down a hill.

The efficiency of these systems is so good that it actually creates challenges. The challenge is there is not much heat being wasted that can be used to heat the passenger compartment. Gasoline and diesel vehicle create so much heat that it is easy to transfer heat into the cabin quickly. With an EV, there is only a very small amount of heat coming from the motor or the battery pack. That means you have to use electricity to warm the occupants when it gets cold.

There are energy wonks out there who think this comparison between the Volt and Cruze is not an accurate enough reflection of the situation. They get all excited about the lifecycle cost of each option. They want to do things like a "well to wheels" analysis of the efficiency. Thank goodness they are doing all of that to keep us on the straight and narrow but it all seems to end up at close to the same place. The companion book to this title, that is called *EVs and the Environment,* goes into those sorts of details.

The other thing about this simple analysis is that it lives where you live. You can buy a Cruze or a Volt. You can buy gasoline and or electricity. It is your choice, if you use the energy involved efficiently or not.

Energy efficiency is one part of what helps these vehicles make sense, but most people really care about the cost. Cost is a more complicated issue and it is discussed in detail in the rest of this book. You may be surprised at how compelling that case becomes when you fit all the pieces together.

Energy Efficiency Matters

Energy efficiency means reducing wasteful expenses. Any household knows the value of cutting waste and almost all businesses need to cut waste for long-term survival. *Why would our individual or national situations be any different with the energy used for transportation?*

The reports related to our dependence on imported oil all point to energy efficiency as a fundamental part of dealing with these concerns. One of the most optimistic reports in this area, the *World Energy Outlook 2012* has the following to say about efficiency:

"Energy efficiency can improve energy security, spur economic growth and mitigate pollution, but current and planned efforts fall well short of tapping its full economic potential."

It goes on to point out that this takes money:

"Our Efficient World Scenario shows how tackling the barriers to energy efficiency investment can unleash this potential and realize huge gains for energy security, economic growth and the environment."

Even if we find more oil or use more natural gas, we will need to use all of our energy resources more efficiently to create a healthy and positive energy future. Electric drive vehicles are a big part of that effort.

Recapture Energy

Electric drives are what give regular *hybrids* like the Prius their great mileage.

Hybrids, and any vehicle with an advanced electric drive motor, recapture the energy they use. Electric drives' recapturing that energy is one of the big energy efficiency advantages. The energy put into a gasoline-sucking vehicle gets a car going and is used up, never to be used again. It gets turned into heat when you hit the brakes. When an electric vehicle uses energy to get the vehicle going, it then recaptures most of that energy when the vehicle slows down.

Driving an EV in stop-and-go traffic around town is an obvious situation for creating this benefit. A less obvious driving condition that recaptures this energy is driving on curvy roads. Speeding up around a curve takes energy and slowing down to go into them gets most of that energy back.

The same energy recovery works with an EV going up and down a hill. The energy put out to get up the hill comes back in large measure when you come back down. This can happen over and over in any hilly or mountainous drive.

Any hybrid vehicle will give you some part of this energy recapture benefit. Normal stop-and-go traffic and driving on curvy roads would get you about the same benefit from a plug-in or standard hybrid.

The *plug-in electric vehicles* have bigger battery packs than the standard hybrids, so they can capture even more energy. This shows up in a really big way when going up and down hills or mountains. With a plug-in vehicle, going up a mountain can take 19 miles worth of electricity and coming back down can take as little as 7 miles worth of electricity. These numbers are used because they come from a real-world experience that has been repeated numerous times. It could be fun to go into the geeky details involved. Ask me about that some time. Here are the geeky things most of the readers would benefit from knowing.

The energy recapture is all done through the process of *regeneration* when the motor turns into a generator. This happens as the gas pedal is released or the brake pedal is pressed. This effect is talked about as *regenerative braking* or "regen" for short.

Regenerative braking is a process that can be anywhere from fifty percent to eighty percent efficient. That would mean that at least fifty percent of the energy put into speeding up the vehicle would go back to the battery when it slows down. The energy being recaptured is called the *kinetic energy,* which is the energy of a mass in motion.

The typical efficiency numbers range from sixty to sixty-five percent and depend on the technology being used. Over eighty percent is pretty impressive and only advanced technology companies make that sort of claim.

This may sound too good to be true to everyone, unless they get the part that all vehicles lose a really big amount of energy to other things. The two big items for an EV are the wind and road resistance. All the items that reduce the range of a vehicle also use up energy, as discussed in the sections on mileage and range in Chapter 12, *Basic EV Consideration.*

Congestion

Traffic congestion is one reason people are thinking about EVs. The more stop-and-go driving you do the more fuel you can save with an electric drive. EVs help with traffic congestion and gridlocked streets for three reasons.

1. Stop-and-go traffic trashes the fuel efficiency on ICE vehicles, but electric drive vehicles barely notice the difference.
2. EV drivers stopped in traffic do not have a running engine so they do not have fumes to get all around and inside the vehicle.
3. Electric vehicles have a quiet, vibration-free ride that is calming and allows for relaxing and enjoying good sound systems when locked in traffic.

All three of these reasons apply to any electric drive vehicle, including regular hybrids, the plug-in hybrids, as well as any kind of battery electric.

Congested areas also tend to have characteristics that support the use of all-electric vehicles. There are EVs in the mix that can save large amounts of time as well as fuel in congested situations. Congested conditions can result in at least three qualities that support EV use.

1. The congestion pushes people toward driving less and driving shorter distances, putting them comfortably within EV range.
2. The congestion means slower travel rates, so less expensive, limited speed EVs become more practical.
3. The congestion encourages the use of two-wheel vehicles like bicycles and motor scooters, which can benefit from having electric drives.

Congestion is not something that is going away anytime soon. It is growing and spreading. It sneaks up on one area after another. People think one heavy traffic day is unusual and then there is another and another. Eventually, they finally realize that they live in a congested area. The sooner we adjust to it, the better off we will all be.

The issue influences us differently, depending on where we live. In Los Angeles, it is a huge issue - particularly in the desirable living and working areas. Almost all the bigger urban areas are experiencing much the same thing.

It has been less of a problem in less intense places like Kansas City. Ten years ago, people in such places would talk tongue in cheek about their commute MINUTES when others would talk about commute HOUR troubles. Kansas City is probably up to commute half-hours and climbing at this point.

Congestion is not some local issue. This is becoming a seriously crowded planet. The population has gone from around 3.5 billion people in 1975 to over 7 billion in 2011. To put that in perspective, it is estimated that it took until the beginning of the twentieth century to get one billion people on the globe. That is 5,000 or 6,000 years from the time we figured out how to start living in cities. The population has increased by over sevenfold in just one hundred years.

Congestion is a global issue that is one of the sources of global pressure to deal with changing our transportation system and increasing the efficiency. As the crowding continues, so does the competition and demand for fuel. That translates into spiraling price increases that you can avoid or at least delay with an EV.

Impacts on Effective Travel Time
Congestion is not just an issue of gridlock and freeway parking lots. It influences the effective travel time under all sorts of conditions.

It has become somewhat amusing to watch how this works out just driving across town in heavy traffic. The vehicles that people drive are all capable of going 80 mph plus. They have huge engines and weight more than two tons. And yet these are what people drive on surface streets all the time.

It is an interesting exercise to ride relatively slow moving e-bicycles or e-mopeds or even a 25 mph Neighborhood Electric

Vehicle (NEV) around town. This gives a different view of how people handle traffic lights. Fast moving cars rush past a slow vehicle only to brake hard at the red light ahead. A 25 mph rider eases up to the waiting cars just as the light turns green and off everyone goes again. The cars go off in a big rush just to wait at the next red light.

It gets even more fun during heavy commute traffic. Cars will roar off the line to get a half a block away to join a three-block-long line at a busy intersection. A slow moving two wheeler will pull up to the end of the line and easily slip down the long rows of stationary vehicles to get to the front of the line.

Then the light will change and, you guessed it, the lead cars roar off in front to get another half-block so that it can happen all over again. It is possible to have a car pass a two-wheel vehicle many times in a relatively short distance. The cars get up to 30 or even 40 miles an hour between lights. However, the reality is that they are traveling the same speed as the bike, which is less than 20 mph.

EV Smile

You are watching the same car roar past you at 30 mph for the fourth time in less than a mile. Sure enough, the light up ahead is changing to red and they will get to do it again.

The cars and trucks are rushing to a red light in their $50,000 vehicles burning $4.00 per gallon gas only to have an electric bicycle glide past on seriously cheap battery power.

This sort of situation has been going on in other countries for a lot longer than in the U.S. That is why those countries are using City Cars (discussed below) and have higher usage rates for bicycles and motor scooters, etc.

You can ride all sorts of two-wheel vehicles through traffic like this. The thing about congestion on surface streets is that you do not benefit that much from having a fast gas-powered motorcycle or motor scooter. You cannot use their speed or range effectively, so why not use the cleaner quiet electric version.

There are lots of people that view driving a bicycle between rows of cars as a little hardcore. It can be, and then again it does not have to be that intense. When the cars are literally stopped, they pose virtually no danger. E-bikes are a nice quiet ride that has a calming effect. It is easy to ride at reasonable speeds and hear any car accelerating. As soon as the engines start to rev up, the e-bike rider slips back into the line of traffic.

Electric versions of these sorts of vehicles can be affordable and operate with very seriously low fuel costs. Not only that, but gas motorcycles can poison a whole line of cars with the smelly exhaust - not to mention the noise!

One part of your EV decision comes from the degree to which congestion is impacting the way you drive. It is very fuel-efficient to use an EV in heavy congestion. The EV solves the pollution problem that goes with heavy traffic in pedestrian areas. The congestion issue will also impact your choice of the best type of EV to use.

Hardcore EV Drivers

The lane splitting concerns brings up the issue of having to deal with hardcore driving experiences with EVs. The concern is that the new technology will create problems.

Most of the old-time EV veterans have had one or more hardcore experiences. They make good stories - like the time I had to push my 300-pound electric motor scooter home for three miles, uphill, in the snow, sort of thing. OK, it was only two miles and a beautiful sunny day, but you get the idea.

The good news is that we are past that learning and experimental phase of things, so you do not need to go there anymore. The new generation of EVs has more advanced technology that is brilliantly executed and you have experienced people to guide you through this without having to get hardcore. But hey, if you want to go hardcore and try to expand the technology and horizons of EV usage, then go for it. There are lots of creative things that have yet to be tried with this new technology. Some of my friends are doing that and one or two of their stories may crop up in your reading.

Chapter 9

Guide to Types of EVs

Electric vehicles come in all shapes and sizes. Most of this book focuses on the vehicles suitable for driving around a city while transporting people. There is however a wide variety of EVs from Segways (two-wheeled personal transporters) to huge trucks capable of moving ocean shipping containers.

The varieties of electric vehicles out there fall into specific groups. These groups have definitions tied to them and help people to figure out which ones are suitable for their use. There are also all sorts of acronyms involved. This section will handle the acronyms and sort out the hybrids and the other EV types more clearly for the rest of this book.

Electric Car Basics

An electric vehicle is distinguished by having two components. One is a set of batteries for traction and the other is a plug-in charging system. There is a third component that they all have and that is shared with a range of other vehicles. That would be the electric drive motor. *Hydrogen vehicles, hybrids without plugs*, and several other categories of vehicles also use electric drive motors.

Most EVs have another distinguishing feature called *torque*. This is the ability to turn a tire really quickly. If a little horsepower is added to a lot of torque, the result is a really quick-acting car. Torque makes many EVs very sporty. They will in fact have a button to press to get a sportier ride. The Chevy Volt actually labels their fast settings as *sport mode*.

Turn that on and hit the accelerator and the car will disappear from a light that just turned green.

EV Smile
It comes from the feeling after you punch the "gas" pedal for the first time in sport mode and watching cars fade behind you. Correction, this can happen for the first twenty to thirty times and every so often after that.

Another distinguishing feature of an EV is a really smooth quiet ride. The electric motors do not have many moving parts, so the noise factor is minimal as are the vibrations.

EV Smile
Driving through your favorite scenic alternative route, you realize that there is only wind and tire noise with almost no vibration. This smile builds slowly as you come to appreciate the quiet smooth ride.

EV Categories and Acronyms
One term used for EVs is *battery electric vehicle* with the acronym *BEV*. This term has been used for many years, going back before hybrids came into the picture. It has been primarily used to talk about the full speed plug-in all battery electric cars. Well, *hybrids (HEV)* and *plug-in hybrids (PHEV)* have batteries and electric drives. So do golf carts, *Neighborhood Electric Vehicles (NEVs)* and two-wheel electrics. Clearly the older term (BEV) brings some confusion with it.

David Sandalow, Assistant Secretary for Policy & International Affairs U.S. Department of Energy, pointed this out at the EVS 26 industry gathering in 2012. He has asked that we start using the name *All-Electric Vehicles (AEV)* in place of Battery Electric Vehicles (BEV) to describe a full speed plug-in all battery electric car. This book will use the AEV acronym and it is comparable to the older use of BEV.

These vehicles are categorized with a number that helps sort them out. This number is based on how far the vehicle can drive on a full battery charge. Most of the AEVs on the road have an EPA rating that is around 80 miles. These are referred to as *AEV 80s*. The 300-mile-range Tesla would be an *AEV 300*. The table below lists currently or soon to be available AEVs by their range grouping.

All Electric Vehicles by Range Grouping

	Seating Capacity	Top Speed mph	EPA Range	Power in kW	Time to Charge	Time 0–60
AEV 40						
Scion iQ EV	4	70	38 miles	NA	4 hrs.	NA
AEV 60						
Mitsubishi i-MiEV	4	80	62 miles	49 kW DC	7 hrs.	<9
Smart fortwo E- Drive	2	83	68 miles	55 kW DC	6 hrs.	13
Transit Connect EV	varies	75	56 miles	52 kW AC	8 hrs.	NA
Volkswagen E-Up!	3+1	84	E60–80 mi.	NA		11
AEV 80						
Chevrolet Spark EV	4		82 miles	104 kW AC	7 hrs.	<8
Fiat 500e			87 miles	82 kW AC	4 hrs.	
Ford Focus EV	4	84	76 miles	107 kW AC	4 hrs.	NA
Honda Fit EV	5	NA	82 miles	92 kW DC	4 hrs.	NA
Nissan LEAF	5	89	75 miles	80 kW DC	4-7 hrs.	11.9
Volkswagen E-Golf	5	87	90 miles	85 kW		11.8
AEV 100						
THINK City	2	70	100 miles	NA		NA
Toyota RAV4 EV	5	100	103 miles	NA	6 hrs.	<7
Wheego LiFe	2	70	100 miles	60		NA
AEV 200						
Tesla Model S	5		208 miles	270 kW AC	10 hrs.	
AEV 300						
Tesla Model S	5	120	265 miles	270 kW AC	12 hrs.	5.6

Primary Source: http://www.fueleconomy.gov/feg/evnews.shtml, additional data from company web sites. Price and other specifications subject to change and may vary. Please use the links at the end of this chapter to check on the current status.

There is another term used when talking about EVs. This would be the "City Car" or a *City AEV*. These would primarily be used on surface streets with only the occasional short trip on the freeway. These vehicles have specifications that result in a lower cost vehicle. This includes a limited range, meaning getting up to a 65 mile range per charge, or having a drive train powered for street use and not so much for freeways. The AEV 40s and 60s, like the Mitsubishi MiEv and like the proposed Scion and V.W. models, are oriented this way, as are some of the others with less powerful motors. That might put the Wheego and the Think City into this group.

These vehicles deal with a modern urban setting very well; particularly when there is a high degree of congestion and limited parking. When the congestion extends to the highways and the freeways, the City Car aspect becomes a moot point. That is because a freeway speed of 50 mph means all the cars are being driven as if they were a City Car.

At the other end of the spectrum, there are the higher range vehicles which include the Tesla Model S and Model X. These are offered with different levels of ranges at varying prices. The basic Model S package includes 208 mile EPA range for a price that starts around $70,000. The top Tesla Model S package includes 265 mile EPA range for a price that starts around $95,000 and more depending on specifications. There was third, entry level Tesla Model S but it is not currently available. Tesla quotes higher range numbers for these vehicles than these EPA numbers, but the Tesla figures are for driving at 55 mph.

The Tesla options are the capital intensive solution that gives wide travel options in an incredibly hot vehicle.

Too Sexy for Your Garage
Some of the EVs look really hot. That really helps get people interested. *Can you handle the heat that goes along with owning one?*

Men think that a sexy car involves speed, power, noise and exotic looks. EVs have all of these going for them, except the noise. There is, however, a real question if it is these qualities that makes a car alluring.

The thing that really makes a car appealing is when women think they are arousing. When women show excitement about a car, then guys will want the car so they can capture a woman's interest. Sorry ladies, guys are just that simple and focused. And yes, you really do have that much influence and then some.

It happened with the Corvette and the Camaro. It has happened with any fast, expensive car. Even if women do not actually think a car is glamorous, the vehicles are sold by creating that illusion. Hence the car ads with hot models all over them. This is the short skirt, low cut top, women in high heels sort of sexy and it works.

Well, the EV world is not showing up with bikini-clad models so much as really well-informed, good-looking and capable women.

If women want to own a car, then that makes it sexy as well. *How else can you explain the proliferation of the SUV?* It may be more of the good provider, solid protector of the family kind of sexy, but sexy nonetheless.

Vehicles like the Nissan LEAF fall into this category. They let the women in a family feel like they are doing something worthwhile as they drive around without spending a fortune on fuel.

This also happens with the Mercedes and Lexus sort of tempting car, only that is evening gown and tuxedo sexy. Put a woman in a Fisker or a Model S and throw in a man in a Tux, and even James Bond would turn his head.

EVs will become sexy when the women of the world decide that they are. If lots of women think that EVs are captivating, then the guys will want to drive them.

This means that any female readers can be doubly effective in helping to get more EVs on the road. The one they get will encourage any admirers to get one also.

There are a good number of women who are working on making this the case. Some of the most well-informed and intelligent people in the EV community also happen to be very attractive and interesting women. They include the *Bay Watch* star Alexandra Paul and women like Linda Nichols who looks marvelous in her red hot Tesla Roadster (one of the first off the assembly line). Chelsea Sexton, the feisty red head in the group, adds passion to her knowledge and intelligence. All three set a high bar for women everywhere.

How Sporty Is the Volt?

Part of what makes a car hot is how sporty it drives in comparison to other vehicles. The Volt is a really fun car to drive but - *how do you describe it or compare it to another car?*

The first thing that gave me a pretty good idea of where it fell in the world of sporty cars was a drive through the mountains. It was a drive I take reasonably often to get home from church. The last seven miles or so are downhill along a nice winding road. The kind a sports car driver really likes.

The thing that made this day different than others is that two cars pulled up behind me just as I was starting the downhill stretch. One was a two-door Porsche and the other was a current generation Ford Mustang with a race trim. Here was a perfect opportunity to see how the Volt drives.

Fortunately I know the road well, so things were reasonably legal almost all the time. There are three or four stretches where a sports car can take off and enjoy the curves. The first curve that I hit the pedal on, both the cars disappeared from the rear view pretty quickly. They caught up on the non-curvy bit reasonably easily as I slowed to a safer speed. The last three curvy bits all went about the same, except the Porsche kept up. The Mustang stayed with us until the curves got tight and it would fall back.

Then came the passing lane and the Porsche blew by me, as I had no interest in speeding through that. It was a Carrera. For those of you who do not know, that is a very fast and very expensive vehicle. The Mustang barely caught up to me at the end.

The second chance to compare the Volt to another sporty car came when a free weekend rental came my way and it was a brand new hot red Camaro. It looked super sporty and had a 3.6 liter V6 engine with lots of power and torque. This is the entry level power on this model. I went on a fossil fuel binge for the weekend, justified by the need to do research for this book - of course.

Heaven only knows what you would do with more horsepower than that vehicle had. It was fast and handled well. It went *vroom* just like a guilty pleasure should. My neighbors all got excited. My friends were almost convinced that I had given up on fuel efficiency because that Camaro looked so hot.

The only difference around town is that people look at the Camaro more than the Volt. They do check out the Volt, but only a certain subset does that. This Camaro was very red and it growled. It even goes *vroom*. People seemed to like that. You can break the law equally easily with either car but somehow you are more tempted by the Camaro.

Traffic, it is the great equalizer. *You can't use the horsepower or the off-the-line speed in traffic, so what good does it do you?!*

The rental coincided with a trip to Santa Monica. I was going to go on the freeway until the rental turned out to be the Camaro. It had a sun roof. It was red. I drove the Pacific Coast Highway so I could cruse Malibu. Now I can say I have cruised Malibu in a red Camaro!

Getting to Santa Monica was uneventful. With traffic all the way, only a little *vroom vroom* was in the cards. Getting home was different. The speed details will not be revealed - I am standing on the fifth for that one.

The main attraction was the stretch of road just south of Point Mugu. You have all seen this stretch of road in the car ads. It is the one with the ocean on one side and a cliff on the other. If there is a big rock in the background, it is the actual point in Point Mugu. It is in 73.5 percent of all car commercials. OK, that is a made-up number, but you would all recognize the big rock involved.

I have driven that stretch over a hundred times. At least a dozen of those were in the Volt. Several of them involved testing the handling of that vehicle at speed. It is a great car and takes that stretch better than most vehicles on the road and better than any other I have driven, until the Camaro.

The Camaro had an edge when accelerating around long curving bends in a legally questionable manner. It held the road better. The acceleration did not kick in as smoothly as the Volt, but it was stronger and pulled longer.

That makes a lot of sense given the specifications. The Camaro has a longer wheel base, which helps with high speed handling. It also has almost twice the horsepower of the Volt. Then again, the handling difference was minor compared with the difference in specifications. This has to do with the horsepower rating on an electric motor not being comparable in the same way as it is on an ICE. More on that in a moment.

The Camaro felt like it was a lighter vehicle on that highway.

The next test came on the stretch of road that goes to my church. I know exactly how the Volt handles on that road. That road does not have long fast stretches. The top speed is lower than for the Pacific Coast Highway and the turns are tighter. Here is the interesting part. There was not any real difference in handling between the two vehicles.

The only difference is that the Volt is easier to drive downhill. You put it into the "L" gear and it slows itself down going into the turns. You seldom need to use the brake as the energy pours back into the batteries. You could probably find a setting on the Camaro that would slow it down. However, that would waste more gas and make a load noise to disturb the natives.

How is that possible? A look at the specifications turned up the answers. The difference on the wheel base does not make that much difference at slower speed and the shorter one on the Volt probably helps on tight curves. It turns out the cars weigh close to the same, with the Volt at 3781 lbs. and the Camaro less than 20 lbs. below that. The real surprise came with the comparison of the torque for both vehicles. The Volt puts out 273 ft. lbs. at zero RPM and the max on the Camaro is only five ft. lbs. more and that is at 4800 RPM.

Torque measures how hard something tries to turn. It is torque that helps with curves. Both cars can pull out of a curve equally well. The high amount of torque on an electric motor is what makes it hard to compare them to an ICE. The Volt may have half the horsepower of the Camaro but the torque is what works on mountain roads, up to a point.

Horsepower is brute strength. You need that to get up to fast speeds. You need that to maintain speed going up a hill. Speeding up and slowing down on a hill, you will not notice the horsepower level so much as the torque.

*Is the Volt as sporty as the Camaro? **Almost**!*

The big difference showed up at the end of my fossil fuel binge. I started to head to the rental return and remembered that I needed a gas station. I could even remember where the local one was, despite only visiting it two or three times a year. I filled up the rental and it took 11 gallons. The car had gone 224 miles on over 10 gallons of gas. The Volt went 3,000 miles on the last tank with less than 10 gallons of gas.

Sporty is one thing and sporty with awesome gas mileage is another. You choose - 224 miles or 3,000 (that is, three thousand!) miles on a tank of gasoline.

Hybrid Vehicles

You would not have read this far if you did not have a pretty good idea that a Hybrid Electric Vehicle (HEV) uses more than one kind of drive power. The most common ones use gasoline in addition to electric drive. There are also hybrids that run on *hydrogen* and there are *natural gas* and *diesel* hybrid prototypes around. The original hybrid vehicles included trains. Trains have used a combination of fossil fuel powered generators and electric drive for over a hundred years.

Most people are fine with the added step of plugging a Hybrid Electric Vehicle in to charge the batteries. These are the hybrids that have more batteries than the earlier versions. As mentioned earlier, Plug-in Hybrids use the acronym PHEV.

Technically oriented people like to differentiate between *parallel hybrids* and *serial hybrids*. The difference has to do with how the car is moved by each kind of power. In a parallel hybrid, both kinds of drive power (gas and electric) are connected to the wheels and move the vehicle. The Prius line is primarily this sort of hybrid, as are the newer Ford Energi models. In the other kind, a pure serial hybrid, the electric motor moves the vehicle and an ICE generates power for the motor. The ICE in a pure serial hybrid is not actually connecting to the driveline (meaning it does not actually turn the wheels). Most people do not care about this; they just want the vehicles to work well.

It turns out that vehicle engineers do not really care about this either. The Chevy Volt is a good example. It is primarily a serial hybrid with a gas internal combustion engine (ICE). The marketing people have translated that into a *range extended hybrid,* which has more meaning. It also allows for the fact that the ICE can actually connect to the driveline and move the vehicle.

The ICE on the Volt hardly ever actually connects to the drive-line. It is set up to do this when traveling over 62 mph and the vehicle is trying to accelerate hard. In over 18,000 miles, my Volt has only ever done that twice that I know about. Both times it happened on a very steep and long grade. I was having fun seeing what the car would do. *Would it be able to pass all those ICE vehicles on the Conejo Grade?*

At the bottom of the long steep grade, there were other vehicles doing 70 plus with me. By the middle of the grade, my Volt was pulling ahead of almost all of them. Near the top, I was moving past them all when the ICE motor increased its speed and it connected to the drive-line to send me over the top at the same speed it started at the bottom.

A Chevy Volt may not be a pure serial hybrid, but it sure can take a hill!

EV Smile
You are blowing past cars on a heavy grade, even more so when you get the rush of the range extender kicking in to make that happen.

There is a common idea that the Volt uses the gasoline powered ICE generator to charge the batteries. This is not what normally happens. The ICE is controlled to provide the electricity that the drive motor needs and not much more, almost all the time. There are two ways to tell the ICE to run more than what the motor needs. One is to turn it on and open the hood of the car. The engine kicks in, presumably so it can be inspected and serviced. The second way is to turn *the mountain mode* on while driving with a low battery pack.

Mountain mode is a setting that tells the vehicle to keep the battery pack charged to about one third of its capacity. The idea being that the charge will come in handy when driving over a steep mountain. The trick to using this is to do it BEFORE you start up the mountain. Here is story about why that is important to know and do.

There is an infamous steep climb called the Grapevine that is on the road going from Bakersfield to Los Angeles in California. One new Volt driver has driving on an empty battery pack as he got to the start of the climb up the Grapevine. It looked like a mountain so he pushed the button to go into mountain mode. The vehicle started working extra hard to charge up the batteries. Then it hit one of the toughest climbs around - the Grapevine! Charging the battery at the same time as climbing the grade was a bit more than the Volt was up to, so it slowed to an embarrassingly low speed.

What the driver needed to do was hit the mountain mode button a half hour earlier. He would have had a good amount of electricity in the battery at the bottom of the grade. That charge plus the generator working full time and the Volt would have been over the grade at full speed. He is fully informed now and looks forward to zipping by other cars on his next Grapevine experience.

Go Anywhere a Gas Powered Car Goes
There is a really important advantage to Plug-in Hybrids (PHEVs), regardless of their all-electric range. They can go anywhere any similar ICE vehicle can go. The electric range does not limit the ability to do anything. If the driver forgets to charge, oh well, just burn a little fossil fuel. If someone wants to drive from L.A. to San Francisco, just do it. The Volt will go 380 miles fully charged and fueled *without stopping*. The Prius Plug-in will go 540 miles!

Like AEVs, PHEVs are also categorized by the range of their battery packs. The main categories we have in play are the *PHEV 10, PHEV 20* and *PHEV 40*. The 2012 Prius Plug-in has an EPA rating of 11 miles, which puts it into the PHEV 10 class. The 2012 Volt has an EPA rating of 38 miles, which puts it into the PHEV 40 class.

Not only do they go anywhere, but they get great mileage doing it. The Prius Plug-in is a gas-burning star with 50 MPG on the freeway. The Volt is almost as stellar with 40 MPG on the highway. They have all of the advantages of being efficient hybrids, with battery range on top.

One thing about the PHEVs is that it really takes some mind-stretching to get how awesome they really are. The Volt has 38 mile battery range and gets 40 MPG. How then is it possible to get 3, 000-plus miles out of 9-1/2 gallons of gas! That is a tank full. And yes, that is three thousand miles. Here is a photo to help you get this idea.

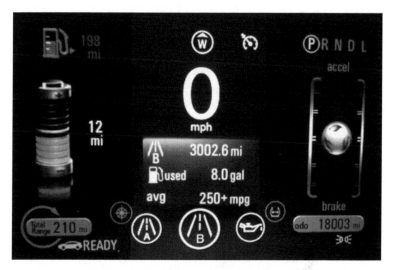

Miles on One Tank of Gas for a Volt

Sorry about this photo showing 3,000 miles on only 8 gallons of gas. I must have missed the 9.5 gallon picture, which would have been about 3,300 miles. This will make more sense as you get to know these vehicles. Just so you know this can be done pretty easily with virtually no hardcore experiences.

EV Smile

You watch the fuel tracking meter turn 3,000 miles before you have used a tank full of gas. Making it to 3,500 miles is even sweeter.

There is one warning about this last EV smile. Someone out there will always come up with an even better story. Like the guy who goes for six months on a tank of gas!

Once you get the PHEV mindset, you will understand why the plug-in hybrid EVs are taking off in sales. There is no fear of being stranded and they are not dependent on public charging for any reason - except convenience and to keep their fuel costs down.

An economically rational PHEV driver will use public charging if the price is right and below what it costs to drive on gasoline.

Converting an ICE into an EV

It can be a lot of fun to pull an ICE out of a car and replace it with an electric drive. These are referred to as *All-Electric Conversions* or *AECs*. There is a whole world of people who do this. It is part of the great American tradition of creating custom rides. There is even a national level society with lots of local groups for people who enjoy doing this. It is called the *Electric Automobile Association (EAA)*. There is a link to connect to this group on the link list.

One thing about doing a conversion is that it is not as cheap as you would hope. There are very few vehicle types that can be converted by hand and end up with a better value than buying a new EV. Electric bicycle conversions can be good values and it is becoming increasingly easy to make affordable electric motorcycles.

It is possible to put together a fairly affordable conversion for use as a City Car. As mentioned above, a City Car is one used around town with only occasional hops on the freeway. They are for driving in a local use area, as they would not have much more than a 30 to 40 mile range per charge.

One thing that helps keep the cost down on a conversion is to convert a vehicle that has lots of parts available. There are some vehicles that have been converted by many people. This, in turn, means people are manufacturing the pieces needed. This saves design, engineering and machining costs. Some of the cars in this group include the Miata, the air-cooled V.W.s, the Jetta and the Ford Ranger.

Converting one of these is a good start but may come with limits. The limits are usually based on budget decisions that tend to go with a conversion. The lowest cost approach usually involves using *DC motors* (a direct current electric motor) with lead acid batteries. These are what can limit the range and performance of the vehicle. They are inexpensive components to get the converted vehicle started and then it can be upgraded as more funds become available.

The older D.C. motors are less efficient going up hills. They also do not have as good capabilities with the regenerative brakes as the newer EV technology. It takes extra work and expense to handle getting regen with DC motors.

The high end conversions involve working with *AC induction motors* and lithium ion style battery packs. One project that some of us in the Sustainable Transport Club worked on used a nice AC motor and two good-sized lead acid battery packs. This vehicle was built for the City of Santa Monica Fleet and has been doing well for over three years now.

One of the champions of the conversion world is a guy who goes by the name of Gadget. You might have seen him in the documentary, Revenge of the Electric Car. He loves the idea of creating really unique conversions out of vintage or specialty cars. One option is to use kit cars like the ones with Porsche bodies over V.W. frames. An MG EV is really fun, as is converting a DeLorean. This means you are creating electric vehicle art that is functional as well. They end up being expensive vehicles along the lines of other custom-built rides that have value way beyond transportation.

Converting a pre-1990s car to electric drive can create a classic look with a 21st century drive train. It gets an inefficient vehicle off the road and stops the high level of pollution that goes with the older engines.

There are companies that can help with doing a conversion and with the parts. There are links on the list at the end of this chapter for both of these.

Conversions can be part of getting serious about using electric vehicles in this country. With a fleet of over 250 million vehicles, it would take a long time to replace them all with new EVs. Converting a few million would help. The cost would have to come down in order for that to happen. The more new EVs that are sold, the better the prices will be for parts. The other thing that is needed is a standardized conversion process so that we can move toward assembly line conversions. This is a good area for entrepreneurs who know how to time the market.

One big advantage is that conversions become reasonably safe vehicles. The original car conformed to the safety standards from its time so most of that advantage stays with the vehicle. There is a safety concern about how well the batteries are installed. The batteries need to be secured in the right location with rugged protection and secure attachments. Locating them as low to the ground as possible seems to help with how the car handles and the crash safety. Leaving as much of the shock absorbing crush zone in the vehicle also seems to be a good idea.

Conversions come close to being as energy efficient as the commercially produced EVs. Add to that the joy of having created an EV and they are pretty cool to have.

Super Energy Efficient Vehicles
The rest of the EVs described below are able to go even farther on a given amount of energy. That means they could be considered Super Energy Efficient Vehicles.

E-Bikes of All Kinds

People can take advantage of the electric drive benefits with a wide variety of other vehicles. AEVs and PHEVs are the ones that can go on any road and operate like a normal passenger car. With the initial investment required for one of those, it is good to have less expensive ways to try out e-vehicles.

Two-wheel electric vehicles (e-bikes for short) are not only tremendously fun; they are ridiculously cheap to drive. Electric bicycles up to electric motorcycles can get a mileage equivalent in excess of 400 MPGe, which translates into fuel costs of less than a cent a mile. That is for rides that weigh 300 plus pounds, so imagine what an electric bicycle does.

EV Smile
You have just told someone you get 400 MPGe on your ride.
They are giving you a blank stare. They do not know what to say.
It is a "this does not compute" stare because they get less than
30 MPG on their car. Go ahead and try not to smile just a little.

E-bikes have at least two niches they fill. One is for people who just love to ride. You know who you are, so just get out there and try an e-bike.

The other niche is for people who live with more traffic than they can stand and they are tired of sitting in lines of cars. An e-ride can be a great choice if you are one such person. Maybe you enjoyed riding bikes or motorcycles back in the day or are a recreational rider now. If any of these apply, then an e-ride could be a great option.

E-bikes really shine in gridlock traffic. The first time you ride an e-bike in these conditions is just a blast. You know the situation. A 15-minute drive turns into 45 minutes to an hour. You could walk faster than the traffic. Imagine gliding down the middle of two rows of stopped cars. If the cars start moving, then you slip into one lane or the other - just to be safe. Sometimes you are on the right side cruising past car after car. You hit an open stretch and you are back in a lane going full speed. The whole car thing stops again and you keep on going. The 15 minute stretch takes you 20 minutes and the people in the cars are stuck for what seems like an hour!

EV Smile

You are driving your e-bike past car after car stopped in gridlock. Your commute takes 8 extra minutes while the four-wheel drivers take an extra hour. Warning: This EV smile situation can be so much fun that you may end up laughing. You might even drive farther than you need, passing more cars - just because you can!

One of the great things about e-bikes is that they are quiet and smooth. That not only works for the neighbors, but it gives a really calming driving experience. It is the sort of relaxing ride that reduces the temptation to do risky things. It becomes more of a sit back while enjoying the sunshine and natural sounds experience. That is in contrast to the vroom, vroom, got to go faster, get out of my way thing that can happen on ICE bikes.

E-bikes could mean any one of the following: *electric motorcycles, electric motor scooters, electric mopeds or electric bicycles.*

E-Bicycles

If riding bicycles is, or was, your thing, then an electric bicycle would let you do more, go farther and commute more often on two wheels. E-bicycles are a great way to get back in shape. The electric power-assist technology of an e-bicycle is one way to overcome many of the problems that keep you from riding a regular bicycle.

The power-assist reduces the pressure it takes to turn the pedals, which can be helpful for people dealing with things like joint or muscle problems. This applies particularly in the hips, knees or ankles. The lower pressure needed can make the activity therapeutic and help to heal these sorts of problems. Even with such concerns, you can climb hills or build up speed easily with an e-bicycle.

E-bicycles make it possible to ride long enough to get to work or run multiple errands. It lets you take the ride while you do only part of the work. The battery pack will let you go from 10 to 40 miles on a charge.

E-bicycles are one of the fastest growing vehicle segments on the planet right now. Sales are hitting the level of 24 million per year worldwide. That is close to the number of cars sold. One e-bicycle representative mentioned that e-bicycles represent EIGHTY percent of all the bicycles sold in Europe! *How long will it take for e-bicycles to catch on here in the U.S.A. to that level?*

California law limits e-bicycles to going 20 mph. That is a good law. There are lots of good people pushing beyond that limit with good reason. The e-bicycle is one of the areas where people are getting hardcore - e-bicycles out there can go 50 mph! At least that is primarily being used at test tracks without any traffic. That is hardcore but with some good sense thrown in. Other riders are putting 5,000 watt motors on bicycles and riding them on the street. This is serious hot rodding, bicycle-style. One guy is pushing motors less than 1,000 watts over 30 mph and riding over 40 miles each way to work and back. Hardcore can be fun but dangerous. Proceed at your own risk.

In the interest of caution, it would be good for a rider to really know what they are doing when going much over 20 mph on a bicycle. If someone has already spent hundreds of hours riding a bicycle with a lot of that in full traffic, then they could be ready for a fast e-bicycle. Taking time to ride at 10 mph in traffic for a couple of hundred miles might be a good idea before going for the speed. Bicyclists are a special breed and keeping them safe is a top priority.

E-Motor Scooters
A good, around town solution can be full-sized electric motor scooters. These look like a Vespa or a step-through motorcycle. They fall into two groups: (1) *electric mopeds* limited to 28 mph and (2) *full-speed electric motor scooters* that go up to freeway speed.

E-mopeds can be a safer ride than a bicycle, and they are a good entry point into the faster two-wheel world. These are more visible than a bicycle with really good lighting. They weigh two to three hundred pounds so car drivers will pay better attention than to a bicycle.

If there are not a lot of bicyclists around your area, then an e-moped might be a good choice. It can keep up with traffic better than a bicycle. The better speed, visibility and weight mean other drivers will be more likely to stay away.

There are a lot of bad boys and girls who are increasing the speed of their e-mopeds the legal limit of beyond 28 mph. The increased speed actually makes them feel safer and probably is safer. It turns out that going 35 to 40 mph allows a moped to keep up with traffic. That reduces tailgating and unsafe passing. This is only hardcore to the extent that it is pushing the legalities.

The legalities are to do with selling such a vehicle that goes faster than 28 mph. The reality is that no one notices the difference in speed driving around town. This hardcore part would be minimized by setting the vehicle back to stock settings before selling it.

E-mopeds are easier to turn and control than a larger motorcycle. Because of this, new riders can get through the learning curve more easily. E-mopeds do not go as fast as their full-speed big brothers so riders will not be able to do stupid things at high speeds. We get to do stupid things at speeds that will have a much lower consequence, thus preparing people for a faster vehicle.

An important factor is to have enough power on the moped. The minimum motor specifications that work seem to be at the 48 volt 2,000 watt level. The batteries are also important as they determine the range. The fact that battery range varies is particularly of concern with these bikes. There is a discussion about that in the companion book to this called *Energy and EV Savings.*

One of the things about e-mopeds is that not many have good quality, good service and/or parts availability. There are parts are available online so all that is needed is to have someone who knows how to work on them to make a go of it. Otherwise, having a stable quality dealer available is an important factor.

The service, parts and power concerns are also relevant to the **e-motor scooter** world. These issues have been behind several of the motor scooter companies dropping off the radar in recent years. Any company that has been in business for more than three years probably has reasonable quality.

The top of the e-motor scooter world is the Vectrix. This is a serious around town and highway scooter. It is incredibly well engineered with good range and well respected quality. The company has been sold to new owners in recent years and is on a firmer footing than before. This is a really quick bike that is a joy for any experienced rider.

The Vectrix can jump on and off the freeway. It has a 68 mph top speed which might not be what is needed for freeway cruising. The larger battery pack (5.4 kWh) has the range for most people's regional area needs (up to 88 miles). These specs make it the equivalent of a basic city motor scooter.

EV Smile

The first time you hit the throttle on a full-speed two wheeler like the Vectrix. OK, it will probably happen the first time you do this on every new full-speed two-wheel ride you try. Really, it will probably happen for the first ten or twenty times you hit it on any of them.

E-Motorcycles

E-motorcycles can be serious transportation that is on par with all of the range and speed considerations discussed for full-speed EVs.

There are several e-motorcycles available on the market, with the most prominent ones being the Brammo and the Zero. These are awesome rides with high levels of technology. They are quick and fast. We are talking serious torque on electric motorcycles.

These companies are already well developed enough that they are way past the quality and parts concerns that exist with the cheaper motor scooters. They are both getting support from lots of levels of government and from the investment world. They have the capability to serve most local and even regional transportation needs.

There is a newer arrival on the market from Mission Motorcycles. This company is doing for e-motorcycles what Tesla has done for the AEV. They are hot, fast and expensive vehicles taking the motorcycle world by storm.

E-motorcycles can get pretty hardcore. There are *drag e-bikes* out there giving gas versions a run for the money. *Dirt e-bikes* can go over 100 mph. *Motocross e-bikes* are getting way out there and *road race e-motorcycles* like those from Mission Motorcycles are setting new records all the time. Seriously fast and seriously hardcore e-motorcycles are becoming a new trend. These hardcore rides are for those who just cannot help themselves, god bless them. That is not something that any responsible writer would actually recommend but, hey, freedom includes the right to self-destruction - so why not do it in an energy-efficient way!

What would be recommended and encouraged is for people to "ride safe" on two wheels.

Neighborhood Electric Vehicles

People who live with certain traffic and driving conditions can use any one of the numerous *Neighborhood Electric Vehicles (NEVs).*

One such condition is for the beach cities that have heavy congestion and parking problems. The traffic flow does not allow anyone to drive fast. There are usually alternative routes for an enjoyable, relaxed 25 mph cruise. Plus, most of what beach people need on a regular basis is within ten miles of home.

Some planned communities have these same characteristics, as do some of the smaller rural cities. People experiencing these sorts of conditions can cut their fuel and vehicles costs to next to nothing by using NEVs or something similar.

Here is how the U.S. Department of Energy Idaho National Laboratory describes NEVs.

"A neighborhood electric vehicle (NEV) is a four-wheeled vehicle, larger than a golf cart but smaller than most light-duty passenger vehicles. NEVs are usually configured to carry two or four passengers, or two passengers with a pickup bed or other utility box that allows NEVs to function as single purpose vehicles such as fire trucks or ambulances.

NEVs are defined by the National Highway Traffic Safety Administration as having four wheels, top speeds between 20 and 25 miles per hour, weigh less than 2,500 pounds (Gross Vehicle Weight Rating), and are defined as "Low Speed Vehicles."

While NEVs were initially used in gated communities, they have been increasingly used by the general public for transporting kids to school, shopping, and general neighborhood trips. NEVs are very cost efficient, in terms of initial capital costs, fuel costs, and overall operating expenses.

In addition to the above uses, many federal, private, and public fleets are increasingly using NEVs at military bases, national parks, commercial airports, and for local government activities. NEVs are reducing petroleum use and simplifying fueling requirements by decreasing or eliminating the need for gasoline infrastructure. For federal fleets, NEVs can help the fleets comply with Executive Order 13149 (Greening The Government Through Federal Fleet and Transportation Efficiency); which requires decreases in annual petroleum."

NEVs are part of the larger Federal category of *Low Speed Vehicles (LSVs).* There are more NEVs than any other type of LSV.

NEVs have another good potential. It is to provide a safe way for people to drive.

A teenager can get used to driving on four wheels in a vehicle limited to 25 mph. Doing that in a gated community with 25 mph speed limits sounds about as safe a learning experience as any available.

Have you ever met a senior citizen who does not have the strength or reflexes to handle a car anymore? Many people in this situation become dependent or use electric mobility scooters to get around. NEVs provide another alternative that is lightweight and cannot hit anything with any speed. That sounds a lot safer than having a ninety-year-old behind the wheel of a 2 ton missile that can go over 60 mph in our communities.

In addition to the resources below, there is a good list of alternative vehicles that might be acceptable alternatives in the discussion on "Family Fleets" as part of Chapter 10, *The EV Mindset.*

Links on Vehicles

Full Speed EVs
BYD Electric Cars   www.byd.com
Chevy Volt
www.chevrolet.com/volt-electric-car/faq.html
Chevy Spark
www.chevrolet.com/spark-ev-electric-vehicle.html
Ford   www.ford.com
Honda Fit
www.world.honda.com/Electric-Vehicle
Mitsubishi i-MiEV
www.mitsubishicars.com/MMNA/jsp/imiev/12/showroom/overview.do
Myers Motors   www.myersmotors.com
Nissan LEAF
www.nissanusa.com/leaf-electric-car/index?next=ev_micro.root_nav.overview
Smart for Two
www.smartusa.com/models/electric-drive/overview.aspx
Tesla Motors   www.teslamotors.com
Wheego Whip EV   www.wheego.net
Commuter Car Company   www.commutercars.com

Neighborhood Electric Vehicles (NEVs)
ACG (American Custom Golf Car) www.californiaroadster.com
BIG MAN   www.bigmanev.com
Canadian Electric Vehicles
www.canev.com/might_e_truck.php
Columbia Par Car   www.parcar.com
Cruise Car, Inc.   www.cruisecarinc.com
E-ride   www.e-ride.com
Global Electric Motorcars (GEM) www.gemcar.com
Lido Motors U.S.A. and Western Golf Cars
www.lidomotorsusa.com/#1

Maya by Electrovaya	www.mayamobility.com
Road Rat Motors	www.roadratmotors.com
Tiger Truck	www.tigertruck.com
Vantage Vehicles	www.vantagevehicle.com
Wheego	www.wheego.net
ZAP	www.zapworld.com

Clean Vehicle Buyers Guides
Lists for more information, including vehicles around the world:
www.afdc.energy.gov/uploads/publication/55873.pdf
www.fueleconomy.gov/feg/evnews.shtml
www.fueleconomy.gov/feg/phevsbs.shtml
www.pluginamerica.org/vehicles
www.edmunds.com
www.driveclean.ca.gov/pev/#

EV Finder	www.evfinder.com

Electric Vehicles UK
www.EVUK.co.uk
www.evuk.co.uk/news/index6.html#Eco_Car_World_2007_Yokohama

Motorcycles and Full-size E-Scooters

Brammo Motorcycles	www.brammo.com/home/
Bravo EVs	www.bravoelectricvehicles.com
eGo	www.egovehicles.com
Electric Motorsport	www.electricmotorsport.com
EMPED EV Mani. Corp.	www.empedscooters.com

EXTREME BIKES
www.ev-propulsion.com/X-Tremeelectricmopeds.html

Hollywood Electrics	www.hollywoodelectrics.com
Mission Motorcycles	www.mission-motorcycles.com
Vectrix USA	www.vectrixusa.com

X-Treme Scooters
www.x-tremescooters.com/index.html

Zapino	www.zapworld.com/zapino-electric-scooter

Zero Motorcycles   www.zeromotorcycles.com

Misc. Other EVs
E-mopeds   www.intragomobility.com/default.aspx
Serious standing scooter www.zuumcraft.com
Arcimoto 3 wheel   www.arcimoto.com
Switch Vehicles   www.switchvehicles.com

Electric Bikes
www.burley.com
www.doglegbike.com
www.electricbike.com
www.electricbikereport.com
www.electricstar.org
www.electricvehiclesnw.com
www.evdeals.com
www.evrdr.com
www.pulseev.com
www.nycewheels.com/electric-bike-reviews.html
www.metaefficient.com/electric-bikes/best-electric-bikes-2011.html
www.bike-eu.com/Sales-Trends/Market-Report/2013/3/European-Unio
n-2012-Is-Cycling-Becoming-Hot-Again-in-Europe-1179947W/

Bike Retailers in the UK
www.halfords.com
www.cyclesurgery.com
www.thecyclestore.co.uk
www.vitaelectric.co.uk

Select EV Conversion Links
Go to www.sustainableclub.org for a full list of parts, batteries etc.
Electric Automobile Association   www.electricauto.org
Canadian Electric Vehicles   www.canev.com
Electric Auto Sports   www.electricautosports.com
Electro Automotive   www.electroauto.com

Electro Vehicles Europe	www.electro-vehicles.eu
Elite Power Solutions	www.elitepowersolutions.com
EV America	www.evamerica.com
EV Drive	www.evdrive.com
EV Power	www.ev-power.eu
EV Propulsion	www.ev-propulsion.com
EV Source	www.evsource.com
HPEV AC motors	www.hpevs.com
KTA Services	www.kta-ev.com
Rebirth Auto	www.rebirthauto.com
Thunder Struck Motors	www.thunderstruck-ev.com
Z Wheels	www.zwheelz.com

Note: These links are provided to help you find information more quickly. Links are subject to change. This is not represented as a comprehensive list. This listing does not represent an endorsement of any companies on this list and there is no business relations with any companies listed (beyond the author purchasing goods and services from some of them).

Chapter 10

The EV Mindset

What will it take for you to claim your Personal Energy Security? For the people who have claimed that security, it took changing the way they think about driving. They looked at the types of things discussed in this book and made the transition from ICE thinking to the EV mindset.

The dominate mindset about vehicles is based on a hundred years of using Internal Combustion Engines (ICEs). In many ways, our lives are built around being able to use these vehicles. Driving these amazing machines defines where we live, where we work and where we buy things, as well as how we spend our spare time. The U.S. and European economies have been made possible by using the cheap oil in these vehicles for a century. All of this creates a way of thinking that is so familiar that most people do not even realize how our lives are defined by these ideas.

The price at the gas pump is going up, as well as the price of oil at the national and international levels. At some price point, it becomes necessary for the dominate ICE thinking to be adjusted to deal with the price increases.

The EV Way of Thinking

The biggest barrier created by people's minds is that they want EVs to do everything an ICE vehicle can do. This puts them into a frame of mind that looks at what an *EV CANNOT DO*. That is a mindset that says the glass is half-empty.

What we need is a glass half-full mindset that asks - W*hat can we do with an EV, and how can we make that work in our* *lives?* Then we can get millions of EVs on the road and start to create oil and energy independence. We can rebuild our economy and national security.

The old way thinks:

- Every car we buy has to be able to go as FAR as the farthest trip we take, even if that is once a year.
- A vehicle should need filling up once a week or every 300 to 400 miles
- It should take about 15 minutes at a gas station to fill the tank.
- Every car should be able to take all the people and as much stuff as we ever fit into a vehicle at any given time.
- The car we drive has to be the same one every day.
- We should only have one vehicle at a time and maybe a bicycle as well.
- Big, heavy vehicles are safer than small ones.

These ideas combine to give the United States the highest per capita use of energy for transportation of any people in the world or throughout history. *Could changing this thinking be the biggest barrier to EV adoption? If so, would that make it a high priority?*

In order to break the grip of these limiting ideas, we need compelling and clearly identifiable solutions. The energy efficient mindset that comes with electric vehicles is one possible solution. The EV mindset involves new concepts about our vehicles that show clearly how the new vehicles and the new lifestyle fit into our world.

The most fundamental concept for alternative fuels is the idea of *having a full tank of fuel every morning.* When charging an EV, home fueling takes the driver less than 60 seconds a day to plug the vehicle in and unplug it. Having that full tank of electricity (OK it is a full battery pack, but we are trying to relate here) changes all the thoughts that go with your use of a vehicle.

The other fundamental idea is that *our vehicles need to meet our daily needs,* instead of doing everything we ever want from a vehicle. Those daily needs represent eighty to ninety-five percent of our vehicle use. The other five to twenty percent of our needs tend to include having many passengers, taking long-distance trips, hauling things with trucks and other occasional special needs.

The new thinking acknowledges *the need to deal with these occasional needs* using new ideas and that can be done in several ways. This separates the need for a 400-mile range vehicle from your daily use. It could mean buying an EV as your first car and using your fume spewing, gasoline-guzzling old vehicle as your second car.

These concepts lead to specific energy-efficient ideas of the EV mindset. These help shift the ICE ideas toward the following:

- The car we drive each day needs to be able to do what we need that day.
- We only need to have one car available for the long trips and it can be a rental.
- We only need one vehicle in our community or family that can take the full crew.

  The rest of the vehicles will take one to four people, as we normally do over ninety percent of the time.

- We only need one vehicle in our community or family that can take the big loads we carry once a quarter.
- It is OK for a household to switch cars, depending on who is doing what for the day.
- One person can have a mix of more than one vehicle.

  Buying a new EV and keeping the ICE is just fine.
  It is OK to have one local use vehicle and one
  full-range car.

- Small and medium vehicles are safer for people outside the vehicle, especially pedestrians and bicyclists.

  They can be just as safe for the occupant as a
  big vehicle.

These ideas can cut your oil dependence by at least seventy percent. It would mean going from 20+ MPG to over 100 MPG. That would end the drain on your bank account, help fix our economy, and do all the other good things that go along with EVs.

Full Tank of Electricity

The ICE mindset involves thinking about how far you can go on a tank of gasoline. Most people want a range of 300 to 400 miles with a full tank on their ICE vehicle.

There are at least three reasons this is happening. One reason is that driving 300 to 400 miles a day is a pretty good measure of a long distance when traveling out of your region. It will get most people from one major destination to the next, at least in the U.S.

The second reason is that many people drive 300 to 400 miles a week. This range means you can fill up once a week and not have to stop if you are pressed for time. So many people are always pressed for time!

The third reason is that the auto industry has figured out the first two reasons and pretty much engineered their vehicles for this sort of range. They then give you information to help you feel good about this so that the norm is established and works.

Part of this ICE thinking is that it will take 10 to 20 minutes to fill up your tank. You may also have to go another 5 to 10 minutes out of your way to do it. That creates an assumption that it takes about a half an hour to fuel your ride.

These ideas have dominated our use of vehicles for over sixty years. They are ingrained as a basic part of our reality to the point that we are not even aware that any other idea might be relevant. These ideas are even used by people developing EVs for market, without trying to shift the mindset. Only people who have lived with an EV for more than six months know just how irrelevant the ICE model is to using any plug-in vehicle. These are the people who have a fully developed EV mindset.

The EV mindset about fueling a vehicle comes from working with the idea of a full charge on the batteries every morning. Veteran AEV drivers are very clear that the important thing is to have a full range available every day to do what they need to do.

EV Smile
Waking up to an 80 mile charge for a typical day that involves driving 40 miles is a good feeling.

It might help people with their head in the ICE age to know that 80 miles a day gives you a week's range of 560 miles. You can travel that far in a week if you have a full charge every day. That is almost twice the range most cars get on a full tank of gas.

Another part of cracking the ICE mindset is to rethink how long it takes to fill your "tank" with an EV. When ICE minds hear an 80-mile range, they think they have to get a fill-up every two days or so, and that means a half-hour per fill-up! It is a subconscious calculation, so maybe the word "think" is a bit strong.

Worse yet, the ICE thinking will ask how long it takes to charge. When this question comes up from an ICE point of view, the frame of reference is a half-hour trip to the gas station. If you answer it takes hours to charge, the subconscious mind knows that is just clearly too long to spend at the gas station!

That sort of ICE thinking can be cracked pretty easily. The best answer is that it takes less than 60 seconds to charge a day. This puts most people who are asking the question into a moment of brain freeze. This is a sign that they are thinking that charging is somehow similar to filling a gas tank. The 60-second answer creates the opportunity to start to shift the ICE thinking.

The next step is to explain that the vehicle is plugged in when it gets home at night. That takes 20 seconds on a normal basis. It takes another 20 to 25 seconds to unplug the vehicle and store the plug. Before driving off the next morning, you would have a full tank of electricity. That comes to less than 60 seconds a day to keep your "tank" full.

Then you say that the rest happens overnight and they are starting to get an EV mindset.

EV Smile
Seeing people get it that charging an EV is quick and
effortless every night.

People will often still want to know how fast it charges. The answer to this is that you set up your home charger so that the vehicle will always be fully charged overnight. The details on "Your Main Charger" will take you through what is involved. Most EVs can set up to be fully charged in 4 to 10 hours with just 220 volt charging so that takes care of things.

The reality is that in less than 5 minutes of your time a week an EV can get enough charge for a range of well over 400 miles, compared to a half-hour stop at the gas station.

One of the EV advocates who is in the documentary *Who Killed the Electric Car?* was the first to come up with an easier way to turn an ICE head around. Her name is Collette, and she is pretty good at turning heads on many levels. She made it simple.

It is just like cell phone charging. You plug in out of habit and your cell phone will keep going.

With an EV, you have even more incentive to remember to plug in. If you forget, there is a pretty good chance you can still do what you need to do for the day (an AEV 80 has enough range for two average days). Forget to do this once or twice on an AEV and you will develop a strong habit. Forget to do it on a PHEV and you may burn half a gallon of gas. Believe it or not, you will have a bad feeling about that!

High-level research surveys have asked people about how long it should take to charge your EV. They are asking people with zero experience using an EV to give an informed opinion. The surveys use charge times of half an hour, 4 hours, 8 hours and so forth. *Is it surprising that people want to spend half an hour or less charging their vehicles?* People are doing that now and why would they want to change! This leads people to conclude that we need fast chargers for people to feel good about EVs. The people who act on that will be very surprised at how many EV drivers will end up hardly ever using these fast chargers, except for regional long-distance driving. *Energy and EV Savings*, the second book in this series, will make that more apparent (See the section on *How Do You Drive?*).

The surveys fail to ask - *Who wants to spend 5 minutes a week dealing with charging their vehicles?* It might have something to do with the people designing the surveys not being EV drivers.

EV drivers get pretty clear about how much they need to charge their vehicles. Volt drivers are using charging stations available to the public more than LEAF drivers. An onsite review of a four-station public charging location showed two LEAFs and two Volts. Three vehicles were charging and one LEAF was just using the premium parking in a busy garage. That LEAF probably was running on sunshine from home charging and the $0.50 an hour fee ($2.00 a gallon gasoline equivalent) from that charger was probably more than the driver wanted to pay. People driving their EVs on solar electricity are paying around $0.50 for a full 80 mile charge.

There is one other thing that EV owners have to do to deal with the 8 to 10 hour charging time. That is to enjoy your evening at home. Eat dinner and breakfast, get some sleep, and enjoy all the other fun stuff you do at home. If that does not take 8 hours, you may need some other sort of self-help book!

Longer Trips

There are days when we travel beyond the all-electric range of our PHEVs and AEVs. We wake up with a full tank of electricity and head out. The EV mindset would also take along a plan to get the charge we need when we are out and about. That plan may include plugging in at work or while having lunch. It might include plugging in at the destination.

EV Smile
***Knowing you have a good plan for taking a trip outside
your round trip range.***

PHEV drivers do this even though it is not necessary. PHEV drivers can go anywhere, so destination charging is not critical in any way. However, it feels good to travel and burn no gas. It is also easy within your local area, as you know where the chargers are and can develop habits that let you use them. Besides, telling your friends you are upset because you drove a 150 miles and had to use a whole gallon of gas gets about zero sympathy. Plus they get tired of hearing about it.

A pleasant side effect is that the charger locations may be such that they are little farther from your destination than more convenient parking. This means that you walk a little farther in order to use them. While this is not always pleasant and EV adversaries will try to use this against them, it has a general advantage. The general advantage is the chance to get a little more exercise and fresh air. Walks that go along the beach or through a park are so much the better. A charge stop in Ojai or Malibu can bring really pleasant walks or even hikes, not to mention access to really nice restaurants and coffee shops.

This trip planning is more important to All-Electric Vehicle (AEV) drivers. There is a discussion in the book *Energy and EV Savings* about your driving habits as they relate to local, regional and long distance. That discussion shows how the driving range limits work.

EV Smile
***Knowing you can make a trip that is twice as far as your battery
range with the charging plan you have in mind.***

Trips beyond a reasonable charging plan for an AEV can be handled in lots of ways. Any household with more than one car has options, and this is a good reason to keep your old ICE vehicle, rather than trading it in.

The important EV mindset concern is not to let the long trip problems keep you from the benefits that an EV has to offer. Have faith that you will find a way, grasshopper (or is that gas hopper?).

Why You Want a Family Fleet

The ICE thinking says every vehicle has to be able to do everything you ever need a vehicle to do.

The EV mindset says that you need to have a way to do everything you do, and that it takes the right mix of vehicles to get that done. That mix of vehicles can be managed with similar ideas that are used to manage a fleet. It can help to think about your vehicles as a personal or family fleet.

Small Fleets have a variety of vehicles the fleet supervisor uses for the various jobs needed. A contractor's fleet might have several pickups, a flatbed truck, a dump truck and working equipment that rides on a trailer. In contrast, a family fleet would have a mix of vehicles for local use, for long distance, for hauling stuff and for special occasions. Working with these vehicles means choosing the right one for each day's travel.

One person can have a fleet as well. Calling it a fleet may be an overstatement when it includes an ICE car, a low speed vehicle (LSV) and an electric bicycle, but the concept works. A larger family might have a PHEV, an AEV 80, a couple of electric motor scooters, an old pickup or an old SUV, as well as several bicycles and e-bikes.

One thing about family fleets is that you do not have to own all the vehicles you plan to use. Rental cars or car-sharing programs can be part of your fleet plan for when you drive long distance. Renting a pickup truck or moving van two or three times a year can be part of how you reduce your fuel costs.

The nature of your family fleet will vary and depends on the right mix for your needs. This not only includes your driving needs but your ability to store the vehicles involved.

Considerations about charging your EV or fueling other types of vehicles also come into the picture.

The family fleet is not going to start out as an all-electric experience. It may have other forms of alternative fuel vehicles. It may always include some sort of fossil fuel burning vehicle, for that matter. Here are some of the kinds of vehicles that can help make your fleet work. Each of these has either an energy efficiency advantage or uses potentially renewable sources of energy.

SUSTAINABLE VEHICLES
Super Energy Efficient Renewable Fueled Vehicles

Bicycles	Miles Per Carbohydrate (MPC)
Electric Bicycles	Over 500 MPGe
Mobility Scooters	
Electric Motor Scooters	Over 300 MPGe
Electric Motorcycles	

High Energy Efficiency Vehicles

Passenger Neighborhood Electric Vehicles (NEVS)	200 MPGe
Utility NEVS for Local Hauling	200 MPGe
All Electric Cars and Pickups	100 MPGe
Plug-in Bio Diesel Hybrids	(under development)
Motorcycles	50-80 MPG
Hydrogen Vehicles	

Renewable or Potentially Renewable Fuel Vehicles

Bio Diesel Vehicles	Up to 44 MPG
Natural Gas Vehicles (Bio-Methane?)	34 MPG
Ethanol Vehicles	24 MPG

In addition to moving toward these vehicles to improve energy efficiency and oil independence, a fleet can fill in specific needs with various alternatives to owning vehicles.

Examples of Family Fleets

The trigger for using the idea of a family fleet came from two of the renewable fuel advocates who have a really solid small fleet. Kent and Cathy Bullard love their LEAF, which they charge with their solar electric system. It allows Cathy to commute with a near zero out of pocket cost for about a 44-mile commute. The LEAF is the vehicle of choice for all their local and regional travel. They have two bio-diesel vehicles. One is a V.W. Golf Turbo-Diesel and the other is a really big bio-diesel Dodge truck. There is also a relatively fuel-efficient Honda CR-V for those trips that would not work for the LEAF and for long distance travel when finding good bio-diesel fuel is a problem.

All of these will have a long service life, so the next step may be a while. Kent is thinking about letting the Honda go. Knowing Kent, he will wait for a bio-diesel hybrid if he can, but he would settle for a Volt.

Another great example is a friend of mine with his wife and teenage boy. They are a good example for beach city situations. The family fleet includes half a dozen bicycles, an electric bicycle, two motorcycles, a minivan and a fuel efficient ICE car.

The electric bicycle serves two functions. One is to commute the seven miles each way to work and back. After a few months, my friend realized he was in such good shape that he did not need the electric assist anymore. The e-bicycle let him get stronger, so now he rides pure muscle-powered bicycles for the commute. The e-bicycle still plays a role as it is used for longer trips around the local area. Trips beyond that range happen on the motorcycle. One of the motorcycles will probably be changed out for an electric version when the price point gets right.

The minivan has the main role of hauling things. The fuel costs on that are a bother so they are looking at the NEV utility truck option. My friend pointed out that these vehicles are a good alternative to a pickup truck. They have a two-person cab and a small flatbed on the back. This works when the hauling is mostly being done around town. A family doing home improvement work, which can get the building materials within a 10-mile radius, would be able to use one of these effectively. The new ones sell in the low teens and there are used ones coming on the market from fleets. That option works for hauling engines, furniture and refrigerators around town, which is about what the family needs.

Between the fuel efficient ICE car and the minivan, they have the sons' driving, the wife's commute and family trips covered. The ICE car is probably destined to be replaced by a PHEV at some time in the future.

One of my favorite family fleets belongs to one of the founding couples of Plug In America. Paul Scott and Zan Dubin Scott were able to keep one of the first generations of the Toyota RAV4 EV they bought in 2002. They had that charging on their solar electric home, and it was a showplace and shining example for many of the EV advocates on the west side of L.A.

That also made them among the first households to drive on sunshine in history. There were only a few hundred highway-capable EVs on the road at that point and only a few of them were charged with solar. Most of the founders of Plug In America are also on that exclusive list of being the first people driving on sunshine. You can see who they are in the documentary *Who Killed the Electric Car?*

The RAV4 was Paul and Zan's primary vehicle for many years. They were positioned to get delivery of the first Vectrix motor scooter in L.A. County, so their fleet started to expand. They still had a standard hybrid car at that point but they did not talk about that much, if at all. The final piece of the puzzle is when they took delivery of one of the first LEAFs in Southern California. Then they were completely on sunshine.

Examples of Personal Fleets
Here is how my mix of rides has developed over time. Fuel-efficient passenger vehicles have been the staple. Bicycles have been part of the mix on and off, depending on the community conditions. When the war in Iraq started to look like it was as much about oil as it was anything, it was time to cut the gasoline use. The next step was an electric motor scooter that was purchased sight unseen from an importer in Florida. It was set to go 28 mph and had a DC motor with brushes. It worked and helped launch the Sustainable Transport Club. Pretty soon, a second earlier version of the same thing was added. That one was purchased used and had been imported as one of the first such vehicles to make it to the U.S. Those two motor scooters, plus the bicycle, took my ICE use from 12k miles per year down to 3k miles.

Both of the motor scooters burned up their DC motor brushes, so they had to be upgraded. At that time, that meant importing bikes and parts from China. Pretty soon, the motor scooters were running around at 35 to 40 mph, using brush-less hub motors and every kind of lead acid battery on the market. These were a great beach city solution that I have used for over 10k miles.

The next move came when the Volt showed up. Out with the all ICE and in with the PHEV. The bicycle is the main ride for the new rural community with two of the e-motor scooters in reserve. The next step is a converted road cruiser motorcycle. That is scheduled for service in the last half of 2013. It will reduce the use of the Volt so that gets to last many years. Plus that ride should get over 200 MPGe on electricity, which is twice as efficient as the Volt.

It would have been nice to be able to have the personal fleet that one of my favorite founders of Plug In America uses. Linda Nichols was a GM EV1 driver. That is the star car in the movie *Who Killed the Electric Car?* It is the one they crushed mercilessly, much to GM's humiliation. With that car torn from her side, she turned to a surviving Toyota RAV4 EV. That held her over until she took delivery of one of the early Tesla Roadsters. It is a gorgeous hot red that looks fantastic.

That story is similar to other founding members of Plug In America, including the man behind the movies. Chris Paine has the RAV4 and the Tesla Roadster and added the Volt as his everyday car. Both of these folks are likely to end up with a Tesla Model S Sedan or something close to that soon. One of the other founders has replaced his original RAV4 with the new version engineered for Toyota by Tesla.

Specialized Vehicles
Here's one big way that ICE thinking becomes energy wasteful. It is when people drive around with only one or two people in a vehicle that they need once a month to take six people around with a bunch of stuff. The same thing happens with pickup trucks that only pick things up once a month. The rest of the time, these larger than needed vehicles are using way more fuel than it takes to get the daily needs handled.

The family fleet can include vehicles that are specifically for those special jobs you need done. If these jobs are done once a week or even twice a quarter, then *why not keep the current SUV, Minivan or pickup truck when you purchase your EV?* Most vehicles will not get much on trade-in anyway.

When you keep your old ICE vehicle and get an AEV, you are effectively creating a two car plug-in hybrid. That is a reasonable alternative to just buying a PHEV. You can take advantage of the fuel savings on your EV and still have your SUV or pickup. There are facts that you can gather to evaluate this, as are discussed in *Energy and EV Savings* in the section on the SUV Dilemma.

There are a few tricks to making this part of the family fleet work. One is to get your next car, the EV, a bit sooner than you would otherwise. The reason for this is that you want to do it while your ICE vehicle is still in the kind of condition that you feel good about. When you shift a vehicle into a special use ride, you will use it much less so it will last many years longer. If it is in good condition when it makes that shift, then it will stay that way for a longer period.

Another trick is to deal with the insurance effectively. Insurance companies will often give a discount for both EV drivers and for multi-car owners. The second vehicle will still cost something, but it will be less than twice as much. It would have even lower insurance costs if your insurance company has a low mileage insurance rate. Low mileage would be something around 5,000 miles or less a year. That is well within reason for this sort of special use vehicle and can save a good amount.

Six months into having a low-use specialty vehicle in your family fleet is a good time to evaluate if it is needed and the best way to take care of it. If it is a keeper, then consider what to do about keeping the battery charged and keeping it clean. In addition, protecting it from sun damage to the tires, paint and the interior becomes more relevant.

Friends and neighbors might consider finding ways to share their specialized vehicles. If one family has a pickup and another has a minivan, they could trade the occasional use. This expands the family fleet into a community fleet that can help keep the costs down for all involved. Have fun with that!

Living with a Local Use Vehicle

All-Electric Vehicles (AEVs) work the best and easiest when used within the local area they can reach without charging during the day. This means charging at home all the time, without having to track down a public charger. Living locally works really well, but it is a challenge to get the ICE age drivers to understand just how well that fits. It fits really well into what you are already doing or could do easily. Living locally can really cut your fuel bills.

One of our EV advocacy groups was working with how best to communicate that and came up with a good phrase that captures the concept. A good name was coined by the Medium Speed EV Coalition. They had discovered how certain communities could work effectively with even a 10 mile radius local area. Seth Seaberg, CEO of Trexa, was the one who put his finger on the name. The solution was the idea of people having *Local Use Vehicles.*

This name captures the strength of AEVs of all kinds with a really catchy phrase. The acronym is part of the fun, after all who can resist driving a LUV. *How does putting more LUV in your life sound as one way to solve our oil dependence?*

The LUV concept is a way to break the grip of touring / longer distance vehicles on the market. Having a mix of long distance and local use vehicles creates huge energy and emissions savings. 100 MPGe cars with zero emissions become a new standard. A household's ICE vehicle would serve for longer distance and faster travel.

The local use question just becomes part of living with your EV. The EV driver has a mindset that says - *will I stay locally today or will a public charge be needed?* If they are driving out of their region, they might consider taking the ICE vehicle instead. *Energy and EV Savings*, the second book in this series, will step you through how well a LUV will fit in your life.

In the early days of EV advocacy, people would talk about getting your EV as your second car. This was an idea to help people get going with the plug-ins and to get past the range anxiety issue. With the new generation of EVs, the tables have been turned to the point that one LEAF driver got all excited when

I mentioned the very idea. They got very passionate that the LEAF was their primary car, and their older ICE was the second vehicle.

It is really clear that if you get an AEV or PHEV, you will want to drive that most of the time. There are just too many EV smiles involved, so people want the EV more than the ICE. The ICE vehicles in your life will become the second or third vehicles.

Living in a LUV Community
What would our lives look like in a LUV community?
Here are some highlights:

- People would use the ultimate Local Use Vehicle (LUV) as much as possible - that would be a bicycle. They would be riding on safer streets with smaller cars and lots of other bicyclists.
- Cars like the LEAF would be operating emission-free for all commutes of 35 miles or less each way.
- Plug-in hybrids could be everyone's main vehicle because they are using all-electric drive when used as a LUV.
- Electric mopeds and e-bikes would be used for short commutes and errands, while the full-range vehicle waits patiently for longer trips.
- Motorcycles and motor scooters of all kinds might be used for mid-range commutes and errands. (The gas-burning varieties would be vehicles with fuel injected, electronic ignition and water-cooled engines with catalytic exhaust so they do not pollute too much.)
- All these LUVs are being used to help make mass transit more effective and efficient.

Getting people around by using Local Use Vehicles is the best thought for an energy-efficient community. Could the people in your community use some LUV in their life!

Getting LUVs into Mainstream Planning

Local Use Vehicles are not supported by the status quo in the U.S.A. Urban development planning does not take the needs of these Local Use Vehicles into account, except in a limited but growing number of communities.

Recent work in Southern California and elsewhere is changing all that. Cities are finding the key role that these vehicles can play. The South Bay Cities Council of Governments has a well- supported discussion of these vehicles and how they fit into planning efforts. The draft update to the General Plan for Santa Monica is another good case in point.

Both of these can be found through the links at the end of this chapter.

Regional Use Vehicles

Trips that require a charge to get an EV home mean you are moving into a wider area that can be called your *regional driving area*. EVs live locally and work well with the occasional trip into the wider region.

What Is Your Region?

The maximum distance each way within a *region* for an AEV 80 would be around 75 miles.

PHEVs like the Volt and Prius Plug-in can handle a region of *any size* without a worry. You would still get great gas mileage, even within a hundred mile range. About the only concern might be a little gasoline anxiety; that is to say, you may be watching your fuel gauge and be a little on edge that you are actually burning gasoline.

An AEV 150 or better can handle almost any region without being too concerned about getting a charge. The AEV 80s would be able to work with a 75 mile radius, get a charge at their destinations, and still get home.

Downtown Los Angeles would have lots of destinations within 75 miles. Santa Clarita with Magic Mountain is in range to the north but not Bakersfield. Most of L.A. County is in the region including Palmdale and Lancaster, however not much of the desert beyond these cities. All of Ventura County is in the region as is all of coastal Orange County down to Dana Point to the south. Parts of Riverside and San Bernardino County can be included out to Yucaipa and Moreno Valley.

Santa Barbara has a good number of community destinations in its 75 mile regional area. This includes Lompoc, Solvang and Santa Maria to the north but not much in San Luis Obispo County. Santa Clarita with Magic Mountain is in range to the east and all of Ventura County to the south along with parts of L.A. County up to about Van Nuys. It would include the coast down to around Zuma Beach.

If your destination is an overnight stay, it becomes easy to recharge as a 110 outlet is all you would need to use your charge adapter. A day trip that lasts 8 to 10 hours can work with a 220 volt charger at the destination. That means you would want to go to the online charger maps to find out where the chargers are located. There is information about charger maps in Chapter 7, under the heading *Links on the EV Solution.*

That points to the other side of this concern. *Are the chargers located in the right place to make getting a charge practical?* The chargers in Downtown Ventura and Santa Monica are just right. You can shop, dine and go to the beach and a movie as your car charges. There is good mass transit to get to other parts of town as well. That is not always the case at all destinations.

The chargers you are looking for include the type that takes all day to charge, as well as the DC fast chargers. The fast chargers will get you an eighty percent charge in less than a half-hour. That would help in the Los Angeles example since there is one fast charger in Riverside and one in San Bernardino. A quick stop there and you would have most if not all of what you need to get back home.

This shows us that we need to get chargers at the right locations. That means one or two chargers at lots of location more than it means lots of chargers in one location. The charger situation is changing rapidly, so anyone interested can track the progress to see when there are enough of them available.

Larger Regional Areas
AEVs like the Tesla and the Toyota RAV4 have much longer distances they will travel on a charge. These are more capital intensive and they may pencil out for your situation as costing less in the long run.

This is the point at which a Plug-in Prius starts to shine. The EPA rating on these says they give you 11 miles of battery electric and then you get 49 MPG on the highway when the ICE is running. The Volt only goes about 40 miles running on a gallon of gasoline. Both of these sound pretty good from the ICE mindset but then you have to run the numbers. The discussion about investing in a Volt in the next book *Energy and EV Savings* goes into these details.

Rentals and Car Sharing

One piece of the EV mindset is that you don't have to own every vehicle you drive. Renting a car for long trips is one way for an AEV driver to handle their travel needs. Traditional rental car companies can make this happen relatively easily. They can also provide the larger capacity vehicles that come in handy when traveling long distance and on vacation. This option works for a week or more away and even for long weekends. They may not be the strongest option for travel that is less than a one-day trip.

Car sharing is becoming a stronger option for short duration vehicle use. A car sharing program is one where people become members of a car-sharing group like Zip Car (Zip Car merged with Flex Car in 2007). Another car-sharing company is IGO Cars.org of Chicago. The companies provide short-term use of vehicles at reasonable rates. The cars are reserved with high-tech tools like smart phones. The system lets the members get a car to drive quickly and conveniently. They are often located right in the members' neighborhoods.

Car shares are most frequently used for 1 or 2 hours. When people need a car for a longer trip, they would then use a traditional car rental company.

The main car-sharing success has been for college students who do not want to have a car on campus. That success has spread to congested cities with expensive parking and storage costs like New York. These programs give people the option of driving the few times they need a car without the expense of owning and operating a vehicle of their own.

These services are becoming more popular and successful. Avis recently purchased the biggest one of these companies called Zip Car. They will be integrating this into their existing network so these services should be available at most Avis offices soon. Most other major car rental companies are also moving in this direction.

Both car rental and car-sharing programs become options for the AEV drivers who occasionally take longer drives. Car sharing works for the driver who needs more range once or twice a month for short periods. They drive by the car-sharing place and, in a few minutes, are on their way for a 180-mile one day trip.

Here is a list of the alternatives to owning vehicles that can help make life with an EV work for all your needs.

ALTERNATIVES TO OWNING VEHICLES

Rental Cars and Trucks
Car-Sharing Companies
Mass Transit Including both Buses and Trains
Re-Localization of Your Life and Community
Access through Proximity
Renewable Fuel Vehicle Rentals

Links on the EV Mindset

South Bay Cities COG reports in beach cities
www.southbaycities.org/projects/electric-vehicles/ev-resources
The LUV discussion starts on page 33 of the report.

City of Santa Monica
Land Use and Circulation Element (LUCE) of the City's General Plan
www.shapethefuture2025.net/draft_luce.html

Data collection system for EV evaluation within a fleet
www.FleetCarma.com

Car Sharing Info
www.carsharing.us
www.zipcar.com
Chicago   www.igocars.org
New York   www.carpingo.com

Chapter 11

How EVs Fit

How does the type of community you live in influence your choice of EVs? The level and type of traffic as well as the parking or vehicle storage, the charging availability, and the distances you need to travel all influence your choices.

There are a whole range of different types of communities with different transportation needs and characteristics. These have been researched and tracked over a number of years. The research has involved studying, visiting and living in these various communities, so much of it involves firsthand experience.

There is one really big variable that needs to be considered, in addition to the characteristics described below. It is the extent to which a city has hills of any significance. Hills make a big difference, so they are discussed at the end of this chapter as a modifying consideration.

Congested Cities

There are an increasing number of cities that are too congested to support the use of individual cars. This happens when the population density combines with the limits on the roads' capacity and the prohibitively high cost of real estate for parking. This combination makes cars too expensive for the majority of people. These factors make travel by car less efficient than many other alternatives. The pollution from high concentrations of cars in areas with high concentrations of people is increasingly unacceptable.

New York, Paris and London are some of the many cities that have made substantial adjustments to these conditions. Others are still working on this, including Mexico City and most of the cities in Asia. An increasing number of cities across

North America are moving in this same direction, particularly in the central city areas.

A description of what has happened in London may help you with your plans. This will be particularly helpful if you live in a congested city or if your city is rapidly moving in that direction.

In the 1950s, the transportation in London worked very well. It had a great subway system that let you get across town easily. The tube (meaning the subway) and the buses could get you around your local area effectively, and driving across the city was pleasant and smooth. Getting out of London was a little tricky, as the motorway system was not fully developed. That was substantially solved by the end of the 1960s.

The city population grew steadily from the 60s on. The population density increased with more high rises and increased housing costs, resulting in turning more single-family homes into higher density flats. The communities that were once out of the city started to merge with the main metropolis. This meant that there was no relief from traffic for miles. Fortunately the people were aware enough of this issue to create a green belt area around the city. This broke up the sprawl and contained the urban expansion to some degree.

As the population grew, all of the transportation systems became more crowded. The surface streets slowed down and the tube became congested. Gradually the parking became impossible, and the popular destinations had a bad combination of gridlocked traffic emitting fumes with pedestrians and bicyclists moving all around.

The full-speed surface rail lines became increasing important during this period. These make it possible for people to get into London from up to 200 miles away for a daytrip. The public transportation then makes it possible to go wherever you need to go once in the city.

The current situation is that there is a consistent condition of near gridlock in the center of London. This is a particular problem in the area of Parliament, White Hall and The City. It persists out to Kensington, Chelsea and to the West End and beyond.

The city of London has created an area that requires a driver to pay a daily *congestion fee* to enter. You have to register before you drive in or you will be fined. The area is surrounded by a system of cameras that track your license against the permits.

Enter at your peril, which means a ticket in the mail and they are not cheap. The standard fees are substantial being close to $20 per day. When you add the permit fee to the expensive parking and the near gridlock, the system becomes a strong deterrent for driving into the core city.

The good news is that electric vehicles get a one hundred percent discount on the fee. The zero emissions mean these vehicles are not poisoning the locals. There is also a concern that emissions impact the architecture and increase the erosion of the statuary. There are reports that this program is providing some level of relief and allowing for basic functionality in the central areas.

There was an analysis of this situation by the Vectrix motor scooter people. They came up with a total cost of driving inside the congestion fee area of close to $100 per day for less than 20 miles of driving. That compared to riding their electric motor scooter at less than $7 per day for the same distance.

The question then becomes what alternatives will work. The city of Paris (France not Texas) had a similar experience, and they did a study to find out what the most effective method of transportation would be to help deal with this sort of problem. They did the study in the middle of the first decade of the 21st century and the findings were remarkable.

The fastest way to get around Central Paris was on a bicycle. Not a bus, not the metro - but a bicycle.

Research Expedition to London
A research expedition to London went about investigating how things are working out in that city. The top deck of a double-decker bus was chosen as the primary research platform. This was chosen in part because an all-day pass would allow a reasonably thorough review of the situation. In addition, several days of traveling on the tube and "minding the gap" were included. For those of you yet to take such a research trip, the tube is the subway and "minding the gap" is a colloquialism for do not fall down between the train and the station platform.

The research turned up a number of good pubs, art galleries and historic sites but that is another story. This does however show that just thinking about London causes my English tongue-in-cheek sense of humour to come out when thinking about research expeditions!

The subway evaluation turned up a number of interesting results. For instance, the system was so crowded that just moving about the stations was challenging and somewhat claustrophobic. There was more stale air than ever before. The platforms were significantly crowded, as were the trains. That would sometimes mean having to wait for two or three trains before boarding. The trains would get delayed due to the heavy traffic and problems on the older lines. Clearly the effectiveness of the underground system was compromised. OK those results were not that interesting.

The more interesting subway result had to do with a very interesting and fashionably dressed young woman. Alas, it was her *folding bicycle* that held the attention. She was spotted 50 yards from the entrance turnstile with the bike on its wheels. She stopped and, in less than 2 minutes, the bicycle was folded to the size of a suitcase. The bicycle passed through the luggage door as the woman passed through the turnstile. She had to stand at the back of the platform before entering the train but that worked just fine. Presumably she had made it to that station much faster than her pedestrian counterparts and would have been just as speedy at the other end of the train ride. A fuller report would have verified that but following her could have appeared more creepy, stalker-like than James Bondish.

Folding bikes are all over the place in London. They can be taken on all forms of mass transit there but were primarily seen on the trains and the tube. The most popular folding bikes being sold include the Brompton, the Mezzo and the Dahon. There is a claim that the Brompton is not only the best but the original folding bike.

Folding bicycles make a good solution, but having large numbers of them on already crowded trains may not work that well. There are two other bicycle options that make a good combination with mass transit systems in heavily congested cities. One is effective *bicycle storage* at mass transit hubs and stations.

Another solution was developed in places like Amsterdam and adopted by both Paris and London. Paris was among the first major metro areas to implement a *bicycle sharing program* based on the results of their transportation efficiency study.

Bicycle sharing has been demonstrated to be effective in places like Copenhagen, Amsterdam and Lyon (France). Paris took this to a new level with 20,000 bicycles put on the road. London has followed suit and now this is a trend sweeping across the planet. Wikipedia has more of those details though the URL provided at the end of this chapter.

This sharing system works by giving people bicycle access from special racks located around the city. People can take a bike from one and ride around an area. They then return the bicycle to any of the special racks and they are done. This allows people to use mass transit to get to a general area and use the bicycle to get to their final destinations quickly and affordably. It not only relieves the burden on the mass transit system but improves the effectiveness for the transit rider.

The research from the double-decker in London showed just how effectively the two-wheel options perform. There were several gridlock situations where bicycles, motor scooters and motorcycles were zipping through the parking lots that were supposed to be roads. Once out of the near gridlock, the overall traffic moved consistently but slowly as the bus moved away from the downtown areas.

Between 20 to 30 mph range motor scooters and motorcycles would filter through the stopped traffic and then get ahead of larger vehicles. Traffic that would get up to 20 mph would be filled with two-wheeled rides. These kept up with the cars and buses as they moved and then kept going through the bigger vehicles when they stopped. That put the two-wheel vehicles many stoplights ahead of the bus within a few minutes. The traffic eventually got up to 35 to 40 mph. The two-wheel vehicles either kept up or caught up at the traffic lights at that speed. Only when traffic got up to 40 to 45 mph, did the bigger vehicles start to get past the smaller two-wheel rides. By that time, the people on two-wheel vehicles that started with the bus in the heavy congestion were already home getting warm by the heater.

There is no accommodation for bicycles on the buses.
Why you ask? Because: *the bicycles are just as fast as the buses in most places!*

The tube is still generally the fastest way to go any real distance in the city. This is true, even when changing trains once or twice. This works because the trains are very frequent. The tube, however, can be a stuffy crowded experience and the trains are subject to increasing delays.

How EVs Fit into Congested Cities

These cities cover large areas and have different conditions, depending on how close a location is to the center hubs. As the location moves away from the inner city, you have the high density regions that surround the center. A little further out and you have the surrounding communities that have more bedrooms than businesses. Each of these would have different needs for EVs.

Inner City
The inner city would have the most expensive vehicle storage costs and the lowest need for a vehicle to get to work or for other daily needs. Many people can just use public transport including taxis. *All-Electric Taxis* are a viable option for these areas, as they drive shorter distances and spend a lot of time stuck in traffic. *Electric Buses* are also being explored and developed for these situations, with China making the most progress.

Increasing numbers of people are turning to bicycles in these areas. Electric bicycles expand the number of people this works for. The electric bicycle makes it easier to ride longer distances and deal with hills. The electric assist means you do not sweat that much, so you can wear your "dress for success" cloths and still look good when you get to work.

E-bicycles are a little heavier, which can make storage a little more challenging. Storage with a charging outlet might also be a challenge. Removable batteries help on both these counts and let you charge them in your home or office. Removing the battery makes the bike easier to lift and to position it for storage or transportation.

Using a NEV (neighborhood electric vehicle), e-mopeds or e-motorcycles in an inner city would require a parking space with a charger outlet. It may take some effort to get that to happen in your city, and it becomes an infrastructure issue. It is a worthy cause as the space of parked two cars can get be used for three

NEVs or for up to ten motorcycles. Motorcycles and motor scooters can be parked in places that cannot be used for a car due to the size and shape. They do not need as much electricity to charge so that part helps as well. The last part of this book has discussions on multi-family and workplace charging that will be relevant to people interested in this sort of option.

Close to the Inner City

The parking and charging requirements for the smaller four-wheel EVs may be more easily met in the areas immediately next to the inner city. Those locations would allow such vehicles to enter the inner city and return without having to charge. The vehicles would also allow access to the bedroom communities surrounding the city.

The areas close to the inner city are prime targets for vehicles that fit the City Car description. These are small subcompacts that are easy to park and can share the road in congested conditions. The smaller footprint helps in heavily congested areas and the range would work for many people.

The even smaller and more affordable NEVs, micro-cars and heavy quadricycles (a European designation) can work in these areas as well. A heavy quadricycle is a step up from a NEV toward being a micro-car. It is very similar to the medium speed electric vehicles (MSEV) discussed in more details in the next chapter called *Basic EV Considerations*.

Both the City Cars and vehicles at the quadricycle level have shown up in lots of cities in China, India and Japan. They were also gaining in popularity in London back in 2007. Some of the first EVs to show up in any numbers were these sorts of vehicles. Around London, they were seen primarily in the areas that surround the inner core including Hampstead and Saint John's Wood. These were the G-Wiz cars, which are subcompact all-electric cars that go 40 to 45 mph with enough range to work in a congested city like London. The vehicles are produced and used more extensively in India.

Surrounding Communities

The less dense bedroom areas would have more room for full-size EVs and their charging stations. The people in those areas would be able to use any EV to good advantage. They are also more likely to need a full-range vehicle that can drive away from the city to other regional destinations.

These areas would also be able to work with full-speed e-bikes to access the inner city. The bedroom areas may also have sufficient storage, charging and parking capacity for each home to support a family fleet. Both of these are discussed in the sections on other types of communities in this chapter, including the one about *Beach Cities*.

The speed of traffic favors different modes of travel. Here is a table that lays out the best way to get around when congestion hits specific levels:

MOST EFFECTIVE VEHICLES UNDER CONGESTED CONDITIONS

Average Speeds	Traditional Rides	Electric Rides
0-20	Bicycles, Mopeds	E-Bicycles, E-Mopeds
20-30	Motor Scooters	E-Motor Scooters, NEVs,
30-40	Buses, Motorcycles	MSEVs, E-Motorcycles
Over 40	Cars, Motorcycles	AEVs, PHEVs, E-Motorcycles

*MSEVs are Medium Speed Electric Vehicles, and they are discussed in Chapter 12.

Car Cities

The appropriate vehicles may be different for cities that were built after World War II. Newer cities were built with the car in mind. These are created using the grid system that goes along with cheap energy. This not only means they are built on a square grid but that grid has wide streets with a system of main arterials, subarterials and residential streets. The square grid is only interrupted by hills, rivers and the areas built in previous eras. These are specifically designed for full-sized vehicles to drive at specific speeds. The bigger the street is the faster the speeds.

The freeway system has been added to connect all parts of the city at top speed. The main arterials connect the rest of the grid to the freeways.

This setup dominates the western half of the U.S., and all the newer areas of pretty much any city, including newly constructed areas all over the world.

Everyone has experienced this and most people consider this the norm for recently developed cities. It works up to the point when it is overwhelmed by too much traffic.

Most of Los Angeles is built this way and is a good case in point. The San Fernando and San Gabriel Valleys are classic areas for this design. They worked beautifully for twenty years or so. Then choke-points showed up getting to downtown L.A. and over the hills to points south. More and more congestion developed, until the actual speed of travel started to drop. Now the efficiency is seriously compromised and the fuel use is rising just as the fuel prices are increasing.

The ultimate expression of this car-centered design can be found in the newest large cities like Phoenix and Las Vegas. Massive arterials crisscross the newest parts of these cities with 45 to 55 mph traffic in three, sometimes four lanes in each direction.

This design is awesome on one level because it creates huge areas with organized access for vehicles. On another level, it creates a serious issue. The serious issue is that it only works when everyone has access to lots of affordable energy. That was fine in the era of cheap energy but that era has come and gone.

How EVs Fit Car-Centered, Cheap Energy Grids
The near term answer for using EVs in these car-centered cities is very simple. Use a full-speed AEV for local and regional driving. It could have two wheels (e-motorcycles) or four wheels but it needs the speed to keep up on these roads. PHEVs will let you do the longer distance driving. Having one each - an AEV and a PHEV - in a two-car family and you are good to go.

Using any vehicle that goes less than full speed creates a real safety challenge with the cheap energy grid layout. Slower speed streets can get you to the local supermarket. Going much farther means crossing the faster streets and that really cuts into your travel time. Many of those crossings have a slower traffic light cycle and do not provide pedestrian- or bicycle-crossing safety measures. Those are the same safety measures you would use for the slower speed EVs. It makes it really tough to justify such vehicles under these conditions.

This does not mean that we should give up on using super energy efficient transport for these cities. It means that there is a need for retrofitting these places so they can accommodate bicycles and e-rides, etc. Creating bicycle and pedestrian routes can be done within the grid. The place to start is along waterways and rail lines or any local feature that reduces the amount of cross traffic on a useful bike route.

One nice safety feature includes bridges and elevated pedestrian/bike paths. The city of Santa Clarita has such a system that works really well with pedestrian/bike bridges throughout the commercial area.

Another good focus for this sort of retrofit is to focus on safe routes to schools for kids on bicycles and on foot. There is a whole movement in that direction with lots of good ideas and support available. This idea is being promoted by children's health and fitness programs that are part of the effort to deal with obesity.

Putting bicycle lanes on roads with very fast and active traffic does not get the job done. This works if the speed limit is 30 mph or less. Much over that and it becomes a high-risk situation. A better option is to create a bike path between the sidewalk and the parking area for cars. This has been used effectively in Europe and the city of Long Beach is trying that as well.

Beaches, Resorts and Ancient Cities

There is something special about a beach city that makes them well suited to electric vehicles. Cities like Santa Monica and the ones in the South Bay Area of Los Angeles all have the same elements in common, and these are also found in the beach cities in San Diego County and many of the ones in Orange County.

The key is that you can get everything you need within a reasonably short distance. The beach communities have all the standard things like groceries and drug stores. They also tend to have farmers markets. The beach part means people go to these cities for fun in the sun and stay for the good food and wine. That means good restaurants as well as cultural events and entertainment. The desirability of being near the ocean attracts people in the upper income ranges who create jobs in the nearby areas. This all adds up to having lots of things to do and being able to get your needs met without having to travel very far.

The other thing about the beaches is they tend to have congestion. This is created by lots of people wanting to be near the beach, combined with limited road capacity. That is due in part to the fact that these beaches were developed early in the growth cycle of Southern California. The roads were put in place before the Second World War in most places, which was before the Gods of the Freeway took control of planning.

Another part of this is that people living in the area are very likely to have a bicycle. Getting to the beach means dealing with parking, so the locals can benefit from riding their bikes to the ocean. This has resulted in good bike paths along the beach, which is another good reason to own a bike. Add the good weather year-round and the foundation is very strong for bicycle riders. In this scenario, one thing leads to another. People start riding bikes to the store and the farmers market, and then you have a bicycle advocacy base for these cities. Bicyclists have to deal with tailpipe emissions, which are pretty much in your face on a bicycle. This makes bicyclists inclined toward considering zero emission vehicles.

Finally, beach people see the changes that are happening with the oceans. They see the sand going away and experience the increasing need for protection from the ocean. Most of the fabled beaches in Malibu have experienced this level of change, with long stretches that have gone from wide areas with sand dunes to places that need protective sea walls and even major stretches of imported rock to keep their homes safe. This is becoming a very personal and expensive climate change experience.

It seems that these considerations are working in beach cities in other parts of the world. Another expedition to the south coast of England turned up similar situations in the beach cities like Brighton. This suggests that the beach city receptivity to bicycles and EVs may be universal. Clearly this needs further research. Sponsors for future research expeditions to the south of France and the Australian coastal cities are welcome to get in touch to help further this research. We could even put a full expedition together and go in force!

How EVs Fit Beach Cities
The first thing is: everything that happens inside or next to the beach city can be done with ANY EV. This includes everything from e-bicycles up to full speed AEVs. One great thing about using e-bikes is that you can store them even without a garage and all you need is a regular household plug to use them. They will go in hallways or in the 5 foot space between buildings. If there is an outlet there, then all you need is a way to keep the charger dry. You can use any e-bikes with that minimal setup. If you are on the ground floor, you can plug in through a window as long as you or any other owner is good with that. If a plug is a problem, then try an e-bicycle with a removable battery. Those batteries can be charged inside your apartment.

One choice is between using an e-moped and an e-bicycle. They will both do what you need in a beach city. The choice depends in part on how bicycle-friendly a city is. A bicycle-friendly city is one with alternative routes for bicycles that do not have cars and trucks traveling fast. They have good wide bike lanes and one or two bike paths. A bike path is a dedicated two-way route for bicycles and pedestrians. They happen along beaches, along waterways, and along railroad tracks easily and effectively. Some cities will even close off side streets and turn them into a bicycle only road. That is a bicycle-friendly city.

The other part of a bicycle-friendly city is how the drivers act toward the bicyclists. If most drivers slow down and give bicycles a wide clearance when passing, then you are at the friendly level. This happens when there are lots of bicycles on the road and drivers see them all the time. This seems to put bicycles into drivers' brains so they see them sooner and get used to driving respectfully.

The e-moped would be a better choice for cities that are still working on becoming bicycle friendly. E-mopeds are bigger and more visible so motorists will see them and avoid them more. They are big enough that these vehicles will damage a car pretty badly and that registers with even unfriendly drivers. E-mopeds are also faster, so they keep up with traffic, and motorists are less likely to try to pass them.

The other advantage to an e-moped is that they are a little easier on your work cloths. You can even ride in a suit and still look good at work. Not so much with an e-bicycle.

One thing to look for is how fast people are driving. In Santa Monica, there is only one road that has a speed limit of over 35 mph. Some of the 35 mph roads have people rushing around at 40 or 45 so they can spend more time at the next red light. These conditions will influence your choice of ride as well as the route you use to get around.

A bicycle-friendly city with these traffic speed limits will let you use vehicles like e-bicycles and 30 mph e-mopeds effectively and reasonably safely. With the speed of these rides, you are best using bicycle lanes and slower speed routes. The routes may have a slower speed limit but you will be almost as fast getting across town due to the congestion on the main routes.

The e-bikes and e-mopeds will reduce your time and stress over using a car. There is less hassle with traffic and parking is cheaper. The 2 to 5 extra minutes you spend getting to your destination will come back to you. You can park more quickly and closer to where you are going than you would with a car. The fuel costs are negligible as well. They both are more physically engaging and you will feel more vigorous with these rides in reasonable weather. E-bikes are a great way to get regular exercise and to get back in shape.

Most of what people do when living and working in a beach city happens within a 10-mile radius. Riding 10 miles to and from work or from shopping is a really effective means of transportation. If that sounds too far, then use the electric version until you realize you are in good enough shape to handle the ride without that help.

Another way to get around effectively is with a NEV (Neighborhood Electric Vehicle). This only needs a driveway with an extension cord for storage and charging, so that part is reasonable. They officially only go 25 mph, which is a bit slow even for congested cities. NEVs would be best used on alternative routes, which are the same ones bicycles would use. Bumping them up to 30 or 35 puts them into the Medium Speed Electric Vehicle (MSEV) category and allows them to keep up on most 35 mph roads (see the discussion about affordable EVs in Chapter 12, *Basic EV Considerations*). They provide more safety and weather protection than most two-wheel rides and you can travel with family and friends more easily.

These options are very effective as long as your road conditions are similar to those described in Santa Monica. Checking the speed limits around town and observing the congestion will let you verify that. If there are routes that go faster than 35 mph, then that needs to be considered. The first consideration is if there are alternative routes that have the 35 mph or lower speed limit. A second consideration is if these alternatives cross faster roads. If they do, *can you cross them safely and in a reasonable amount of time?* Waiting for a lot of long cycle lights to get across fast roads will reduce the effectiveness of the slower speed EVs, even in congested conditions.

A good beach solution for when the roads are a little faster is to go to a full-speed e-ride, like e-motorcycles or e-motor scooters - instead of the e-bikes or the e-mopeds.

Faster EVs will work as long as you have a way to park and charge them. The slower ones are generally smaller and work about as well when the roads are slow and congested. Plus, they are less expensive.

Beach dwellers do leave the beaches from time to time. It is tough to do that for most died in the wool coasties, but they do it anyway. People in Santa Monica have a sense that they want to live most of their time west of the 405. People in Venice go so far as to want to stay west of Lincoln Blvd, but that seems a little over the top.

Leaving the beaches can be done in a number of ways. The most common way includes a full-speed vehicle with enough range to drive to all your regional destinations. AEV 80s and e-motorcycles can do that in many situations. Evaluating that is discussed about how you drive in *Energy and EVs Savings*. PHEVs go everywhere so you already know they are a viable option.

Express mass-transit is another option. Taking any of the EVs to the train station or bus depot will open up many of the regional destinations more effectively than taking local buses. There is a whole discussion about how this works, based on research done by the South Bay Cities Council of Governments (SBCCOG). The web address for that report can be found at the end of the previous chapter, *The EV Mindset*. The report has good information about all of this, and it is a good resource for planning professionals and energy efficiency advocates.

The density of the beach city will determine if a car-sharing program would solve this need or not. With lots of people and high costs for parking, there is a good opportunity for these programs to work. Car sharing is discussed in more detail at the end of the previous chapter.

University Towns

University towns are another special case. Universities towns seem to create characteristics in common across the U.S., as well as in parts of Europe. This adds up to favorable conditions for electric vehicles of all kinds.

The university town is one that is primarily built around the campus. They tend to have a limited size and a reasonable separation from surrounding areas. Classic examples include Davis and Isla Vista in California as well as Oxford, Cambridge and York in England.

These cities are some of the *premier bicycle cities* in their countries. They are also becoming some of the *best EV cities,* at least in the U.S. Clearly we need another sponsor for a research expedition to verify this in other parts of the world!

This is happening for a number of reasons. It would be a good bet that students and faculty have figured out the need for energy-efficient transportation, and it is probably more than just that.

Another part of the reason has to do with the layout of these towns and small cities. Part of this is that the size and layout of the town puts everything within the ten to twenty mile range that favors even entry level EVs. The university is typically the main activity center for the town. This means that people will travel from most parts of town to this destination. This results in lots of bicycle infrastructure with bike paths, lanes and parking, as well as secure storage. The bicycle friendly elements help with using e-bikes of all kinds. They can also support NEVs which are a preferred option for bicyclists as they do not spew fumes or drive too fast.

In England, the York train station has the most awesome bicycle storage. It is a sight to behold, with at least three hundred bicycles, motorcycles and motor scooters lined up in a large area under a roof. The whole area is right next to offices staffed with station personnel who keep an eye on the area. The next research tour will clearly need to include another trip to York to see how many electric vehicles are in that area.

The idea of a research trip to the university towns is not just because they are fun to visit; there really is a need for the research! It can help us learn more about building EV and bike friendly cities. So what if they are filled with really interesting people, great restaurants, high levels of culture, etc. Research teams can learn to adjust to those sorts of conditions!

These cities often grow with the main business district adjacent to the university campus. In California, the cities of Davis and Isla Vista grew up along with the adjacent colleges. In York, the whole thing goes back a lot further and the businesses were built up by people going back to invading Vikings. The businesses were next to the castle, the cathedral was next to the castle and the university snuggled in for safety.

Regardless of how things got going, the net result usually means that the downtown is accessible by local use vehicles like bicycles. In the case of Isla Vista, there are some services right next to the campus and a whole world of culture and recreation in the adjacent Santa Barbara. The local use vehicle culture has spread to that whole region and the two cities are well-linked by a bus system. They are close enough that any electric drive vehicle with a 20-mile range can access the whole area.

How EVs Fit in University Towns
Here's the bottom line with these sorts of communities. The people living there can do everything they need around town with any sort of electric vehicle - from the electric bicycles up to electric trucks. The only reason to own a touring car is to get out of town. Even then, there is often train service that will handle that part for you. All you really need is a vehicle at the other end of your train ride.

Weather conditions become a concern. Electric bicycles are not that much fun in snow or in rain storms, but an enclosed NEV might be just fine.

Rural Towns

There are many smaller cities and towns with conditions similar to the university towns. They tend not to be as well planned, and the downtown areas do not have the added attraction of a nearby university. This means that it might take a bit more effort to make bicycles safe for the community, but it can be done.

How EVs Fit Rural Towns

One small town in California is a perfect place to use e-bicycles and NEVs. It is the charming community of Santa Paula. Ironically, one of the first two commercially viable oil wells in California was established just outside Santa Paula - making it a prime starting point for the states oil dependence.

People can ride bicycles to any part of town easily. They have a bike path along the rail line that follows Main Street. Much of what people need can even be done by walking. In this setting, an e-bike would make things really easy on two wheels and let grandparents keep up with the rest of the family on bicycles. A NEV would increase the safety and comfort.

One e-ride that does not fit in well in this community is the electric motor scooter or for that matter the e-moped. The added range and safety of these vehicles does not make much difference in a small town. They are too slow to work for driving to adjacent communities. This adds up to there being no real benefit for the extra expense, compared to a decent e-bicycle.

This city does not have everything the locals need. It takes traveling to the nearby communities for shopping, employment, recreation and entertainment. The reality is that an AEV 80 would handle this part almost all the time, without even needing to use public chargers.

Good examples of slightly larger rural communities would be Ventura on the Central Coast of California and Santa Rosa in Northern California. These are large enough that going across town and back on a bicycle is more than most entry level bicycle riders would want to do. The e-bicycles, e-motor scooters and NEVs become relevant at that point. These could work in Santa Rosa because there are lots of different routes with different speeds. If all the routes were higher speeds, then there would be a benefit to upgrading to e-motorcycles and MSEVs for all travel around town.

Santa Rosa is in the middle of a beautiful part of the wine country. An AEV 80 would let people access most of this area. That would include all the wonderful communities like Healdsburg, Sebastopol, Sonoma and Petaluma. All of these are within the 35-mile radius that would make up the local use area for Santa Rosa.

In point of fact, an AEV 80 would allow people from Santa Rosa to take a daytrip to San Francisco and back. They would need a good charger in the city to make the trip home worry-free.

Ventura has a local use area that includes all sorts of interesting destinations. These include everything from Santa Barbara to Magic Mountain and half of Malibu. In between, you have all sorts of great beaches, surfing and hiking.

Surfing

Speaking of surfing, the EV advocates in Santa Barbara report that a Chevy Volt can fit three surfboards and their riders. Michael Chiacos from the Community Environmental Council took a research expedition without even needing a sponsor for the work. His report is in the form of a really big EV smile. Perhaps he would be willing to do a more in-depth analysis in other surfing areas. It would be good to verify that this will work with other vehicles, perhaps a Tesla Model S! Location could also be important. Anyone interested in a research trip to Hawaii or Australia?

EV Smile
Arriving at your favorite surfing spot with two buddies and their boards in your plug-in hybrid EV.

Surfing actually creates a challenge for people interested in energy-efficient transportation. On the one hand, people who are close to the ocean would have some idea about wanting to help take care of the planet. Then there is a need to carry one or more surfboards and the kit that goes with it. That puts them into a dilemma, along the lines of the SUV dilemma mentioned in *Energy and EV Savings*.

Here is the thing. Long boards are fine and give a certain kind of ride that many people prefer. But they become the reason that surfers drive big trucks and SUVs. These people could benefit from reading the companion publication to this book EVs and the Environment. Perhaps then they would go out and buy a shorter board and an EV that will fit the board in it or on top of it.

Hills Make a Difference

Your choice of an EV will change if you live in a city with significant hills. Any cities with hills, like San Francisco and its neighbors, would fall into this category, as would Palos Verdes and Ojai in Southern California. There are these sorts of hills adjacent to many cities, with places like Hampstead in London and Montmartre in Paris as good examples. Let's face it; if you want to ride up to the Mark Hopkins in San Francisco, the Sacré-Coeur Basilica in Paris or the Hampstead Heath you are going to need a strong EV.

Any full-speed AEV or PHEV will be able to handle this, but the other options need to have the right specifications to pull this off. Here are some guidelines about what will or will not work.

First off, real hills mean no NEVs, or cheap e-mopeds or cheap e-bikes. It would be possible to upgrade these sorts of vehicles so they would work. However, that is probably not a good way to spend your money. If you are thinking about upgrading a NEV to handle this, you might consider doing a conversion on a light compact car like a Miata or a V.W. Bug instead. Such a conversion would need more than double the specifications given below for a motorcycle. You would end up with a slightly more expensive and significantly better vehicle.

An electric bicycle is going to need good quality parts with good specifications. Good quality means precision-made with specifications and heat management that keeps them from burning out. Such parts are more expensive but keep you rolling. Most e-bicycles with 500 to 650 watt motors will work fine on flats with the occasional hill. Real hills call for 1,000 watts on the motor. More is better, if your legal situation and sensibilities allow. Bear in mind that some places have regulated power limits on specific types of rides. These are set to try to protect people and often make the new technology unusable in real world conditions as an unintended consequence.

The e-bicycles will also need a strong battery pack. Forget about a lead acid pack; they are just too heavy for hills. A lithium battery pack with something around a 20 amp hour battery pack or better with at least 48 volts would do a good job. The volts are needed for torque and reduced heat. The amp rating on the battery is needed to create the current to get up the hill.

Serious e-motorcycles like the Zero and the Brammo or e-motor scooters like the Vectrix motor scooter would work. A heavier faster motor scooter or motorcycle will need even more of all the items mentioned for an e-bicycle. Most of the faster two-wheel rides get by with 3,000 watt motors or more and that works for the occasional hill. Real hills need at least 5,000 watts on the motor and 10,000 or 20,000 watts is sweet. They will also need a strong battery pack. A lithium battery pack with at least 40 amp hour battery systems or better with over 60 volts would be good. The battery pack would need to be able to put out at least 100 amps for as long as it takes to climb a good hill.

Charging on Top of a Hill

There is another consideration about hills that might impact your use of an EV. It is to do with having your trip end at a destination up a hill. The same concern applies if you plan to use a charger that is up a hill. Going up a hill takes a lot more energy than driving on flat land. This means that you would need to take the extra work into account with your trip planning.

The easiest way is to increase the number of miles you would want to have left when you arrive at your destination. Veteran EV drivers would normally plan to have something around a minimum of 5 miles range by the time they get to a charger. That is a reasonable margin for error. If the charger is up a hill, you might simply adjust that to a 10 mile margin of error. The more you drive, the better you would get at allowing for this factor. If you live on a hill, you would become very comfortable with how much charge it takes to get to your home charger.

Links on EV Use

London Congestion Zone
www.tfl.gov.uk/roadusers/congestioncharging/

Wikipedia on Bicycle Sharing
www.en.wikipedia.org/wiki/Bicycle_sharing_system

LA City Bike Plan
www.labikeplan.org
www.yousendit.com/transfer.php?action=batch_download&send
_id=894177555&email=12fa3a38049ba4450ff2418b19a0c2cf

Motorized Quadricycle
http://en.wikipedia.org/wiki/Motorised_quadricycle
www.aixam.com/en/licence-free-car/legislation
www.smart-trailers.co.uk/twizy.htm

Chapter 12

Basic EV Considerations

This part will provide a better understanding of the driving range and performance issues to do with EVs.

Range Ratings

All range ratings are not equal. This is a really important to know before buying an EV. A range rating is how many miles the EV can drive on one charge of the battery pack. If you base your choice on the wrong rating, you may be in for more effort than you bargained for.

It is an almost universal experience that manufacturers will provide optimistic mileage estimates. They can prove that their vehicles can drive as far as the estimates. *What is wrong with that?* If the idea is to drive on a flat road at a constant speed, there would be nothing wrong with that. That is how many of these vehicles are tested. Different companies will also use different speeds for their testing. This could be anywhere from 20 to 55 mph. Experienced EV drivers will refer to that as a *flat track rating.* Since most of us do not drive that way, it may be difficult to go as far as we expect based on manufacturers numbers.

There are other ratings to be wary about, particularly EV driver boasts. A 100 mile manufacturer rated vehicle can be induced to give 110 miles, 120 miles and sometimes more. The way to induce that out of the vehicle starts by setting all of the performance specs on the vehicle to the most economical. The EV is then driven using every hyper-mile technique, including staying on streets with speed limits of 35 mph or less. There are published reports of being able to get 138 miles out of a LEAF by doing that.

It can be fun to try this once in a while; however for everyday travel, it is a lot of effort.

It is also worth knowing these techniques in case you get into a situation when you are a little tight for a charge to get home.

Here is a look at how much the range can differ, depending on who you talk to, how you drive, and how the car is set up. The eighty percent figure has to do with both a car setting and with DC Fast Chargers as discussed in detail later in this book.

DIFFERING RANGE NUMBERS FOR A LEAF

Nissan Original Specification	100 miles
Hardcore Hyper-Mile Range	138 miles
EPA Range	73 miles
80% of EPA as Fast Charge Max.	58 miles
Range with Lots of Heat or A/C	47 miles

Hyper-mile driving is moving in the direction of being a hardcore EV driver. Then too, it can be fun. Plus, there are times when going into hyper-mile techniques is a good idea. That would include any time you are pushing your ride to the edge of its' range. This means switching from a lead foot to a feather foot, coasting as much as possible, and using maximum regen for any downhill or stop and start driving. There are blogs for EV drivers who want to learn more about this.

What to Do for Real World Range Figures?

The easiest figures to use are the *EPA ratings*. The EPA range estimate is one that is close to what you can expect if the EV is driven at freeway speeds. That means 65 to 70 mph, in case you are one of those that think 75 to 80 is full speed. The tests are done without totally taking wind drag into account. The EV might get slightly less range with consistently fast driving. However, it is not enough to get too concerned about.

There is another nice thing about the EPA range numbers. They are as close as we can get to comparable numbers. The testing is well defined and can be verified for consistent results. That means they provide good comparisons from one EV model to another. There also seems to be a good basis for comparing EVs to gasoline engines, as will be discussed more in other sections.

There are, however, a lot of things that create concerns about the range of electric vehicles. Some of these can be handled with the good data below. There is also the whole range anxiety discussion that non-drivers of EVs get excited about. It may be a surprise as to what a non-issue range anxiety becomes.

There is a basic part of handling range anxiety that will be used throughout this book. That basic part is to be prudent and do all thinking and planning with a margin of error built in. When thinking about using an AVE 80, for example, that margin of error would be to leave 5 to 10 miles as a reserve for dealing with unexpected things that come up. This would mean that even though the vehicle is rated at 80 miles, most trip planning would be based on driving 70 to 75 miles. As people get to know their EV, they will find that some trips can be as long as 100 miles in an AEV 80 - due to all sorts of range changing things like speed and hills. Experience makes the margin of error more manageable.

The margin of error for driving on battery power on a PHEV can be cut down to *zero*. The error with these is simple. Oops, the car just burned a 10th of a gallon of gas to get home!

There is a whole convoluted world of testing standards that some people get into. This involves terms like *EPA's "LA4"* or *"the city test"* or the *Federal Test Procedure (FTP)*. These are for fine-tuning estimates for technically related issues. In the link section at the end of this chapter, the EPA address with the word dynamo-meter provides more information on this level. This is only suggested for the deeply technical and analytic people.

Range Changers

The real-life things we do can totally change the range. The biggest differences in real-world driving are how fast you accelerate, how fast you drive, how hard you brake and how often you brake hard. Tire pressure and type can make a ten percent difference or more. Climate control can be really big, particularly when using a lot of air conditioning. Heating can cut range as the vehicle has to use electricity to generate heat and there goes the driving range.

People who live in places that require a lot of climate control might want to know how this will impact them. The people at the Idaho National Labs have come up with figures to help with that.

The following table can assist you when you are adjusting the range expectations for the seasonal needs in your area.

IMPACT OF EQUIPMENT ON EV PERFORMANCE

Accessory	Range Impact	Comments
Air Conditioning	Up to 30%	Highly Dependent on ambient temperature, cabin temperature, and air volume
Heating	Up to 35%	Highly Dependent on ambient temperature and cabin temperature
Power Steering	Up to 5%	
Power Brakes	Up to 5%	
Defroster	Up to 5%	Depending on use
Other: Lights, Stereo, Phone, Power-assisted seats, windows, locks	Up to 5%	Depending on use

Source: US Department of Energy, Idaho National Laboratory

Clearly the A/C and heating are big issues. ICE drivers also expect A/C to cut their mileage, so that is no big surprise and one that EV people will adjust to easily.

People are not used to having their heater cut their mileage. Internal combustion produces lots of excess heat that is easily directed to heating the passengers. The electric drive motor is so efficient that it does not produce much heat. That means an EV only has a small amount of motor heat available to warm the people involved. The rest of the heating would need to be created using the electricity and that cuts range. The table above about differing range numbers shows how the thirty-five percent reduction calculates out for a LEAF.

Chad Schwitters is a Tesla driver and board member of Plug in America. He points out that the figures for the Tesla would be different due to the large size of the battery pack. The test results shown above were created when an AEV 80 was the standard EV and before the 265 mile range of the Tesla. It would take an extreme set of weather conditions like the one detailed below to use anything close to 35% of such a large battery pack. Here is what Chad has to say about the range on his Tesla.

The worst I have seen in a year of driving was about 183 miles of range in my "265 mile" car; this was going over a mountain pass in January. Not only was the heater going almost full-blast, but the tires were pushing a lot of snow and slush out of the way, and the trip had significant net elevation gain. All of those factors combined still took less than 1/3 off the rated range. I can't imagine a worse case than that, but the car still did a little better than your theoretical 35% deduction just for heating.

The heating factor will reduce the effective range in places with cold climates. This can be offset by heating the vehicle when it is still plugged in. People who live in places like Minnesota are already familiar with this idea. They will turn their vehicle on remotely to get it warmed up before driving. They also heat the engines with electric warmers using plugs available in most parking lots. The home, workplace and public EV chargers will allow people to warm the passenger compartments in their EVs using electricity instead of the fume-producing engines. Some of the vehicles will let you do this with smart phone applications or over the Internet.

There is an advantage created by the engine warmers being used in cold places like Minnesota. They have already resulted in there being lots of 110 volt plugs in a huge number of parking lots. These represent places to charge EVs. EV charging uses more current than the engine warmers, so there will be some challenges but the basics are there already.

There is similar situation with the air conditioning part of this for areas with hot climates. Vehicles plugged into a charging station or even just a 110 volt plug can have their A/C running before the owner is ready to take a drive. This is made possible because the A/C systems work on independent electric motors. The nicely cooled vehicle will be a welcome change to the hot gasoline vehicle that takes 10 minutes to cool off.

This points to an opportunity for people in hot climates. Having 110 volt plugs in a business parking lot would attract EV owners who want to cool their vehicles while shopping. These could be a revenue source for the business.

Of course, some people will start their ICE cars and run the A/C before driving. Then they have to get through the fumes around the vehicle before they get in and hope that none of the toxins get inside.

It is unfortunate that all cars cannot use their A/C in the same way that EVs can. Then again the technology that has been developed for the EV could result in other vehicles being able to so this. If a vehicle shifted to using electric drive A/C systems, then it to could be plugged in. That way, even an ICE vehicle could stay cool without burning gas and creating toxic clouds of fumes while doing so.

This idea is gaining traction as many new vehicles are coming with features that are using names like "preconditioning." This means heating or cooling the vehicle before driving. The connection to using a household outlet to power this may become part of that picture soon.

The many things that impact range become important when starting to drive an EV. That is one of the differences between ICE thinking and an EV mindset. EV people think more about how far they will go, framed in the concept of the range for a given trip. ICE thinking is more about miles per gallon. The things that impact both range and miles per gallon are very closely related. Most of what it takes to get better mileage in an ICE car will help with the EV range.

Then, too, there are things that hurt mileage in an ICE vehicle that may not hurt the range in an EV. An EV recaptures the braking energy and turns that into miles. This happens with stop-and-go traffic, as well as hills - as discussed previously. An ICE engine uses a lot of power to get up a hill and wastes a lot of gas with the engine braking going downhill and on mountain curves.

When a destination is at the end of a long uphill, then the range getting there will be very different from the range leaving there. This is one of the things that new drivers will want to learn about and leave a healthy margin of error during the learning period when driving to an uphill destination.

One of our long time EV drivers has a good and simple way to adjust for hill and mountain driving. What he does is keep track of how many miles a hill costs to climb and how many miles a hill gives back when you come back down. He knows for example that the Conejo grade costs him ten miles to get up even though the grade is about two miles long. He also knows that he gains three or four miles when he comes back down. Using those figures lets him plan his trip and his charging needs.

People who do a lot of mountain or stop-and-go driving might want to make sure the vehicle they get makes *energy recapture* easy. Some vehicles require pressing the brake pedal to get strong regenerative energy recovery. Other vehicles have a mode of operation that provides a good strong regenerative braking when the accelerator is released. It is usually a setting on the gear shift that is sometimes identified as *"L"* for low gear. Other models will use a *"B"* designation to do the same thing.

The other side of this issue is that it is good to have a good coasting ability to get the best range. This is a setting that lets the driver take the foot off the accelerator and coast with almost no slowing and almost no regenerative braking. This gives better range under conditions other than mountain or stop-and-go driving. It is not essential to have this coasting feature, as the driver can learn to coast even on the strong regenerative setups. Most experienced EV drivers would take a strong regen setting over a coasting setting if forced to choose one or the other. It would take a few months of driving an EV to understand why that is the case.

EV Smile
Every time you reach a new level on your battery range because you figured out how to drive more efficiently.

Range Nightmare Stories

There are stories about EVs gone bad and stranding drivers. A now infamous article in *The New York Times* on February 8, 2013 has one of the worst such stories. A reporter took a Tesla Model S out for a long-distance test drive and ended up getting the vehicle towed as it ran out of juice. This is more a good example of an ICE head handling of an EV than of how EVs can work. Going through how that happened will show how to avoid such problems.

The Tesla Model S has an EPA range of 265 miles. Tesla has set up superchargers in specific areas to allow drivers to recharge really quickly at these chargers. The rate of charge is stated to be 150 miles in half an hour. The *Times* reporter took all of these specs at face value and started driving.

The root problem was that the test was done shortly after one of the worst storms in recent years and in freezing temperatures. Freezing temperatures mean that an EV will have to use electricity for two purposes. One is to warm the occupants, which means a thirty-five percent average reduction of range - based on the table above. The other is to keep the batteries from getting too cold when the vehicle is not in use, which means using electricity when parked overnight.

The warming of the occupants would drop the basic range from 265 miles down to 172 miles under average conditions. That is big, but not a problem for regular use. It becomes more of a problem in a situation with chargers spaced 150 to 200 miles apart!

This problem started to show up when the supercharge fill up showed only a 242 mile range. The range calculations on most of these systems provide information about how far the vehicle went, based on recent driving history. The range estimate from a charge would tell the driver something like: if you drive the way you have for the last few charges cycles, then you can expect to go (in this case) 242 miles. Each computer system calculates this in a different way, using weighted averages and fun math like that. There is virtually no way to predict the driving conditions ahead, so predictive errors are to be expected.

One of the details in *The New York Times* story is that the reporter took a side trip into Manhattan. It was a short trip but that could be really slow going in a congested city after a big storm. The total distance could have been as little as 5 miles but it might have taken 15 minutes and included parking for 10 or 15 minutes with the car working to stay warm the whole time. That little trip could have easily used 10 or even 20 miles of range. An experienced EV driver would have put the vehicle on a charger someplace if the trip was for lunch or any stop lasting an hour or more.

This is probably about the time the reporter started calling Tesla and was told to turn the heater off and drive more slowly. Now you have the nightmare of unsafe driving in a freezing car.

The next detail is that the car's computer showed it was not charged to 100 percent at the second supercharger. The meter showed 185 miles and the data recorder showed the battery was not full. The best case reason for this would be due to the charging slowing down as it gets close to being full. That is basic to charging most batteries and is particularly important on advanced batteries, as described in *Energy and EV Savings*.

If it did start to slow down the charge and the newbie uninformed reporter was sitting in freezing weather, then he may well have pulled the plug to get back on the road. An 80 percent charge would have taken approximately 45 minutes at the speed of charge that Tesla quotes for the superchargers. The number of miles would have been approximately 212 under normal conditions. If we discount that for the use of the heater by 35 percent, then we are down to about 140 mile range. That is when the trouble would have really started.

Another detail of the story is that the reporter stopped to spend the night. The car had something around 90 miles of charge at that point. The guy had not read the manual and was not instructed to follow the basic rule of using EVs, which is to plug it in overnight. So the car was left in freezing temperatures with a low charge. It went into battery warming mode and the range dropped to 25 miles by the next morning. Even plugging into a 110 volt outlet would have given him more than a 90 mile range. The net result was a tow truck and a bad report on the vehicle. How ironic that ICE thinking should kill an EV drive due to freezing temperatures.

The moral of this story is to build a well-informed EV mindset before planning a long trip in an EV in the dead of winter, or for that matter in the heat of summer. Oh yeah, reading the manual might help also! A long trip can be done, especially in a great car like the Tesla Model S. However, this is only if you know what you are doing. It is a good thing that you are smart enough to read this book before getting involved.

What about MPG?

Traditional thinking is that fuel economy is tied to the miles per gallon (MPG) on a vehicle. Electric vehicles use electricity sold by the kilowatt hour (kWh). *How do we translate that into MPG?*

Plug-in hybrids have an easy way to bridge the gap between MPG and the cost of electricity. The *Fuel Economy Guide* numbers on the Volt make that almost straight-forward. The Volt takes 35 kWh to go 100 miles. That works out to mean that a Volt would cost $4.20 to go 100 miles, using the national average price per kilowatt hour of 12 cents. It gets 40 MPG when it is running on gasoline. The math is pretty simple to get the cost to drive 40 miles. It would be 40% of the $4.20, which is approximately $1.70 to drive 40 miles. Given that it uses a gallon of gas to go 40 miles, this makes a pretty simple statement possible and here it is:

A Volt gets the equivalent of a 40 MPG car, paying $1.70 a gallon, when driven on electricity and charged at home.

It gets more complicated than that with other vehicles, particularly any type of AEV. This gets handled by using the concept of *miles per gallon equivalent* or *MPGe*. There are official standards for figuring this out, and the following story will show you why that is needed and how that works.

I remember the first time the question of comparing the MPG on an all-electric came up. It was when people wanted to know what the fuel cost was for an electric moped. These mopeds use so little electricity that the cost could not be determined from the monthly utility bill. What it took was using a simple plug-in electrical meter, like the one called a *Kill O Watt*. This showed that these e-mopeds could go about 12 miles on one kilowatt hour. Using the 12 cents per kWh price makes for easy math, such that the fuel cost was about one cent per mile.

The next step was to turn that into some sort of miles per gallon. At the time, the cost of gasoline was fluctuating between $3.50 and $4.00 per gallon. So based on cost, the equivalent was up to 400 MPGe. That sounded too high a number, so another way was used to get an equivalent.

The other way is to compare the energy used. A basic energy measurement is how many BTUs (British Thermal Units) are used with each fuel type. Running these figures resulted in an equivalent MPG of 700 MPGe. *If 400 MPGe seemed too high, then what would 700 MPGe do to people's brains?*

It can be pretty fun to throw out these numbers and watch what people do. There is a brain freeze that happens. Some people get a look that suggests they are having a "This does not compute" experience. It is like they are getting data that they cannot fit into their understanding of the world. It took a good few weeks of going over the numbers before I started using the 400 MPGe figure. It was sufficiently large to get people's attention and somehow seemed more believable.

EV Smile
Realizing that your MPG is way off the charts and it really does cost "next to nothing" to run your vehicle.

MPGe Conversion

The EPA and their *Fuel Economy Guide* use a standardized system to solve the concern about how to calculate MPGe. Their *Miles per Gallon of Gasoline Equivalent (MPGe)* for electricity is the basic energy equation derived from the BTU content of both gasoline and electricity. *The number they use is 1 gallon of gasoline = 33.7 kWh.*

That is probably the best way to keep a standard set of numbers with a solid basis for comparison. This energy comparison method is the basis for MPGe figures for AEVs and PHEVs. These range between 90 MPGe to 109 MPGe for highway driving. Given that an ICE vehicle of is more likely to get between 20 and 40 MPG, you can see part of the EVs energy-efficiency advantage. In the case of a Volt, it gets 93 MPGe on electricity and 40 MPG when burning actual gasoline; the difference being the lower efficiency of the ICE generator.

The cost savings is not explained by this comparison alone. It gets more complicated because a gallon of gas does not usually cost the same as 33.7 kWh. Most people know what they pay for gas but very few keep track of how much they pay for a kWh. That tends to be in the range of 12 to 14 cents a kWh in the U.S. That means that a gallon equivalent of electricity costs $4.04 to $4.72. That is close to the range of prices currently paid for gasoline. The electricity may cost a bit more but it takes a vehicle two to three times as far. This is another look at how the gas and electric prices have converged, as discussed in Chapter 6, *Personal Energy Security.*

As the price of gas goes up, the benefit of owning the electric vehicle will increase. That is, unless the price of electricity goes up the same percentage.

The following table shows how the MPGe works out for different types of vehicles. The numbers are more "typical" than actual averages. Averages are hard to come by as vehicles vary so much.

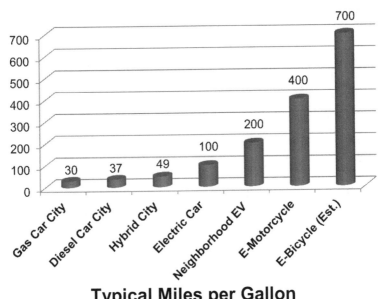

Typical Miles per Gallon
or Equivalent

Energy Efficiency and Super Energy Efficient
The graph above is a good visual statement that using an electric drive motor in a vehicle will increase the energy efficiency involved. Hybrids are the starting point, as they use electric motors to get the better mileage. Clearly AEVs are a strong next step and a plug-in hybrid would be between these two. If these three types of vehicles can be referred to as energy-efficient vehicles, then it makes sense to that getting more than twice the performance from the same amount of energy would be super energy efficient.

Range Anxiety

As mentioned above, the nature of an EV causes people to talk about *range anxiety,* meaning that people will be tense about how far they can drive before they run out of juice. This is something that keeps the ICE mindset in place and causes inexperienced EV drivers a bit of trouble. EV drivers who know their vehicle get past this and the anxiety about range is no more than the anxiety about getting a flat tire. Experienced EV drivers know how to handle the limits of their vehicles.

As Paul McCartney might say - *it's all in your mind love!*

Range anxiety does not apply to PHEVs. They have a gas tank and can drive on gasoline indefinitely - just like any other ICE vehicle. The variation on range anxiety that a PHEV driver has is a form of what the actress Alexandra Paul calls "gasoline anxiety." It goes with thoughts along the following lines:

\-

"Oh no, my batteries are getting low. I may have to burn some gasoline to get home!"

\-

Do not expect to get any sympathy from friends when this happens.

The trick to getting past range anxiety is to replace fear with knowledge. Getting that knowledge is what this book is all about. Here are some tips for moving through the learning curve with range anxiety quickly and without too many problems.

Chad Schwitters points out just how easy it is to deal with range anxiety with a Tesla Model S. Most of these vehicles have a full EPA range of 265 miles so that helps cut anxiety right there. Here is the guidance from Chad:

My advice to newbies that don't understand their Tesla is to not take any trips over 177 miles until they get used to it. I say they should be able to make it 177 miles no matter the conditions. I also tell people to always plan a charging stop after 2/3 of their rated range. If conditions are good, they won't need the charging stop and may continue on, or simply charge for less time than planned. But if conditions are bad, that's a valuable buffer to have! Keeping that 1/3 buffer means that you can drive at speeds you like, with the heater set to a comfortable position, and not worry about making your destination.

Overcoming range anxiety with an AEV 80 can be a little scary for some or it can be a source of excitement. I say, let's turn this into an adventure in greener, cleaner living! This is an adventure of discovery, discovering how your community works in more detail and seeing how to make it a more energy-efficient and a cleaner place to live.

Learning How Far the EV Can Drive
When a new driver starts to use a defined range vehicle, it is prudent to take time to get to know how far it will travel. Here is a list of ideas about how to go about getting familiar with the range without getting into problems. The numbers on this list are chosen for an AEV 80 assuming it starts any trip with a full charge. You can adjust these to match the range of any vehicle you may purchase.

- Start by driving in the local neighborhood with trips of not more than 20 to 30 miles in total.
- Next, try driving to and back from a location that is about 20 to 30 miles away. This will give you an idea of what happens after using up half the range or more. (Hint, just keep on driving.)
- Then take a similar trip and add a few more stops while heading back to the charging station. This will put the batteries into the last third of the charge.

- Try going similar distances to destinations in different directions to get a feel for the size of the local driving area.
- Start to find the charging stations available to the public in the local area and the ones just outside the local area.
- Try a trip that involves charging at one of these locations for an hour or more. See what that means when at the end of the trip.
- Gradually enjoy more of the local area while pushing into the regional area with more public charging.

This is a good way for a driver get to know the limits of the vehicle and what it feels like to run low on charge. A few runs that include lots of hills will expand your knowledge of range. A couple of tests on the freeway compared to tests around town will also expand this knowledge. This knowledge can be used to try different destinations to see how far the vehicle can go. The operator should try to end up near a charging station for what should be the last half or at least the last third of any test drives.

Following these steps becomes part of that adventure of discovery. It provides a good understanding of how great these vehicles are and that they can do almost all of what is needed. Within three to six months, you will be using the vehicle without any concern in the local area. The only concern beyond the local area will be if you will be near a charger long enough to get the juice needed. That may mean enjoying a latte and reading a newspaper at a nice cafe but you might survive that experience as well.

Range Testing

Those who are technically and or analytically oriented may want to conduct actual tests to see how far an EV will go. It might be good to do this after five or ten good trips, as described above.

It is worthwhile to have a logbook to write down the information (see the form in the next book, *Energy and EV Savings*, in the chapter *A Guide to Getting Your Facts*). This logbook can help sort out what kind of driving gets what driving range. It will show how your EV driving habits develop, as well as how the battery is changing.

Here are some steps for a range test.

- Make sure the vehicle is fully charged.
- Make the opening entries in the logbook.
- Drive to a place or on a route that will use up at least two-thirds of the charge.
- Be within a few of miles of the charging station when approaching the two-thirds level.
- Drive the vehicle around in circles that get closer and closer to the charger as the charge fades more and more.
- It would be best to set a lower limit for the test. Five miles or ten percent of charge remaining is reasonable. Different batteries and technology are involved and draining one hundred percent of the charge can be a concern.
- If the vehicle kicks into "crawl home mode," it is time to go straight to the charging station and plug in.
- Write down the mileage at which it hit the chosen limits and/or when it went into crawl home mode, the ending mileage, as well as any other relevant information. It is good to note any drop in the top speed when arriving back at home base.

Here is the disclaimer for this process:

This process will work for commercially developed EVs, like the LEAF and for conversions from ICE to EV with lead acid batteries. The distances used are for vehicles with proven 80 mile range on the packs. Other vehicles would be tested with distances adjusted for the size of those packs. Conversions with any of the many lithium or other advanced chemistry batteries would need more detailed adjustments. The owner would need to know how low to discharge the batteries without causing damage.

Following this sort of strategy will allow an operator to grow in confidence and create a wide circle to work with the electric vehicle.

The best way to handle the concerns of a limited range vehicle is to not need the range. It is a choice between running around town in every direction and planning trips so they require the shortest distance.

Range Will Change over Time

Caution – the range will change over time on any battery pack. The way they change will depend on a number of variables, including the type of battery being used. *Energy and EV Savings* has most of the details and the *Battery Secrets* involved.

What Really Happens with a Limited Range Vehicle...

It can be hard for some people to see how enjoyable it can be to drive an EV that has a limited range. Most people think that a day's driving would involve the 35 miles of charge on a Volt and a few gallons of gas. That idea makes the thought of going 3,000 miles on less than ten gallons seem absurd. A day spent driving a Volt can help make that clear.

The day started in Santa Paula with 36 miles worth of full charge in the morning. It ended in the afternoon with 6 miles worth of charge, after having driven over 68 miles *without using a single drop of gasoline.* Even people with poor math skills will realize that either this is a crazy lie or there is something going on that they do not understand.

The big thing people do not understand is how *opportunity charging* helps make this work. The first leg of the trip was to Ventura, which is 17 miles from Santa Paula. The chargers in the downtown area let me charge while I was at the farmers market and doing some banking and other errands. The next step was to go 15 miles along the ocean to Carpinteria. The charge in Ventura put me up to 31 miles of range. So that was not a problem.

Carpinteria has a new charger at the train station, so the charging began again. A nice walk through the charming old town, along with a couple of errands, and I was ready for some coffee and a little time with a newspaper. When back at the car, I had 32 miles of range. A scenic alternative route home went 20 miles through the enchanted Ojai Valley. It was time for lunch near the chargers in the city of Ojai. After a short lunch, the charge range was then up to 17 miles. That happened to be the distance to Santa Paula so off I went. By the time I got home, I was still on all-electric with six miles to spare.

Oops, there is another math riddle. *How could I drive 17 miles with 17 miles of charge and still have 6 left over?* There are two parts to the answer. One is that the 17-mile range was calculated based on having spent most of the last few days on the freeway. The trip from Ojai is mountain driving, which is slower and gives better mileage. The other part that explains this is that Ojai is at a higher elevation than Santa Paula, so the regenerative braking put a good amount of energy back in the pack.

The net result is that the day cost about $2.00 in charging fees and another dollar or so to charge on the home charger. Not bad for 68 miles worth of driving!

In the interest of full disclosure, it should be noted that this trip involved more walking than would have been the case when driving a gasoline car. That did add more time to the trip. The walking would be between ten and twenty blocks worth of exercise that I need anyway. It was actually one of the reasons for the trip.

Taking this trip in a LEAF would have been even easier – *no charging required.* The other option with a LEAF would have been to extend the day trip with just a little charging here and there. The trip involved a something over four hours charging time. The newer LEAFs can charge twice as fast as a Volt, so that would have provided at least 80 miles with the same amount of charge time. Add that to a full charge to start and you have around 160 miles for a fun daytrip. *How many day trips need more than 160 miles?* All it takes is a charger at two or three places that you would spend time at anyway!

At this point, you should be starting to get how an EV mindset develops and why EV owners are so in love with their vehicles. I think we have found another EV Secret.

EV Secret
"Opportunity charging" is part of what lets a PHEV
get 3,000 miles on a tank of gas.

Creating More Affordable EVs

One of the issues with EVs today is that they are being used by reasonably well off people more than the rest of the world. The question is how to get the upfront cost to come down so that more people can get started. The world outside of North America has found answers to this. Those options are taking time to get on the road in the U.S.

This is a social justice issue, apart from anything else. The government is spending large sums to put expensive vehicles in households that are the wealthiest in the country and in the world. This becomes a situation where government money is being spent to help people who are perfectly capable of helping themselves. It might make more sense to spend that money to help people who actually need some help.

This would mean promoting vehicles that are far less sexy than a Tesla. It would mean looking at e-bicycles and e-mopeds, as well as NEVs and something a little more capable like the Medium Speed Electric Vehicles (MSEVs) discussed next.

Conversions from gas to electric have potential for creating less expensive EVs. There are things that need to happen before that gets easy or has a real price advantage, as discussed in Chapter 9, *Guide to Types of EVs*.

Other countries have a much wider range of affordable EVs available. They are showing up in the categories of vehicles that exist in the range between NEVs and full-speed vehicles. These include super compact vehicles that have a limited speed and limited range on the batteries. All of Asia uses vehicles of this nature. They are using them as the basis for building an electric vehicle industry that is surpassing that in the U.S.

The U.S. is reluctant to go down this path. The main obstacle is the safety regulations set up by the federal government. The effort in the United States to deal with this middle category is being put forward under the name Medium Speed Electric Vehicles.

Medium Speed Electric Vehicles (MSEVs)

MSEVs vehicles are light, small and affordable. They can go 35 mph and are able to travel up to 35 miles per trip. A Medium Speed Electric Vehicle is similar to a micro-car in Europe. England has a designation for a quadricycle that fits in this group.

These vehicles are an answer to the issue of how people can get an EV for a cost they can handle. The lower speed and range means that they need smaller motors and battery packs. This translates into a retail price point at and below the $20k mark, even with low production volumes.

These vehicles are legal in nine U.S. states. They are being sold as advanced NEVs, which means they have safer bodies with doors and bumpers and many other safety advantages over a NEV. Once they are sold, the end users increase the speed to the state-recognized limits of 35 mph to turn them into more functional vehicles.

There is a concern that these are not recognized by the federal government and violate regulations from the National Highway Traffic Safety Administration (NHTSA). This puts them into a similar situation as the medical marijuana. The states will turn a blind eye but you never know if the Feds will do something about them. Fortunately the only thing the Feds can do under the current rules is to go after the manufacturers and anyone who sells them as MSEVs. They could pressure the states to cancel the laws but that has not happened as of yet with the MSEVs.

How much sense does it make to treat the most affordable EVs the same way as a drug? We are addicted to oil not EVs (yet).

The market testing and research effort has been done by a considerable number of people. This includes low-speed vehicle manufacturers, fleet operators in government and private sectors, electric vehicle dealers across the country, and by individual operators of various low-speed vehicles and electric conversions.

The testing and research has shown that there are three basic requirements for an MSEV. The first one is that it keeps up with city traffic. The second one is being able to get off the line on city streets quickly enough to keep ahead of other cars. The third one is that it be able to allow a person to drive 15 miles to work, charge the vehicle and get home with charge to spare so they can run errands. This means the three minimum requirements for the MSEVs would be:

1. Being able to go 35 mph or more
2. Adequate acceleration from 0 to 35 mph
3. Having a minimum of 20 miles on a charge, with 35 miles or better being preferred

The evidence for this 35-mile-per-hour requirement can be found in the nine state laws that allow NEVs to go 35 and the other nine states that are considering such a move.

The problem is that safety regulations do not allow viable MSEVs into the market easily. The companies involved have to go through safety testing designed for full-speed passenger vehicles. There are thirty-eight safety specifications for passenger vehicles. New producers can meet around eighty percent of these reasonably easily. The expensive components include elements tied to crash testing.

Limiting the speed to 35 mph means these vehicles have five safety advantages over heavier and faster vehicles as follows:

1. They have some of the lowest destructive energy of any vehicle that drives in our neighborhoods.
2. Their limited speed is in the speed range with the shortest possible braking distance.
3. Less than twenty percent of all fatalities occur with vehicle speeds below 35 mph.
4. The zones with speeds up to 35 miles an hour are the safest of all speed zones, with less than twenty percent of the accidents happening in those zones.
5. These vehicles cannot exceed the speed limit. Meanwhile speeding vehicles contribute to 37.5 percent of the accidents in these speed zones.

Adding all of these up will show how there is a clear safety advantage to a vehicle that can only go 35 miles an hour. Over one-third of the fatal accidents in 35-mph zones are tied to speeding vehicles. Since an MSEV cannot speed it will cut fatalities accordingly. With only twenty percent of fatal accidents occurring in the slower speed zones that means a 35 mph vehicle could reduce its exposure to only two thirds of those accidents or less than 15 percent of all fatal accidents. Limiting a vehicle to going 35 mph in 35-mph zones could keep that vehicle safe from over 85 percent of all fatal accidents. *What other safety feature can do that?*

What the NHTSA is overlooking in blocking these vehicles is that having MSEVs on the road would reduce the number of the more dangerous vehicles and eliminate the option of serious speeding. The MSEVs would not be as big threat to bicyclists and other bike riders, not to mention pedestrians. They are also significantly safer than bikes of all kinds.

The NHTSA's narrow focus on resolving safety issues by adding technological gadgets is encumbering our ability to resolve other pressing problems. They are ignoring the benefit of reducing the mass and speed of the vehicle on the road when it is mass and speed that creates the basic and most lethal safety hazards in the first place.

Releasing Creative Potential
The federal government is the main body that can release the creative potential of free enterprise.

There were close to thirty manufactures in this country that were positioned to produce MSEV vehicles. However, they have been constrained by federal regulations. Removing these constraints would allow these Medium Speed Electric Vehicles to develop rapidly and start to solve the high cost of EVs. Unfortunately the constraints from the government have combined with the recession and the arrival of the AEVs and PHEVs to create a perfect storm of conditions that have hit the manufacturers pretty hard. Many of these companies have pulled out of the business and jobs have been lost along with the potential for affordable domestically produced EVs.

The big thing that would release the creative potential of these sorts of companies would be a classification for a Medium

Speed Vehicle (MSV). The right safety specifications on this MSV class of vehicles would allow vehicles of all fuel type to flourish as city cars. It would take the brakes off this development and put people to work, creating a green jobs solution to our energy and pollution issues.

That is why we need to get the NHTSA to create a new vehicle classification. That new classification would spell out the federal safety standards needed for this group of vehicles.

The NHTSA was petitioned by various parties to create this classification and they denied the petition. It has since come to light that the NHTSA is funded by the National Highway Fund. That fund gets over half its revenue from taxes on gasoline and other oil-based fuels. (Yes, the rest comes from the general fund, meaning your income taxes.) It would look a lot better for that agency if it got on board with supporting more energy-efficient technology and renewable energy options than continuing to play a big role in increasing the size of vehicles with the accompanying fuel increases.

This MSV class of vehicle would foster the development of electric vehicles. It is also ideally suited to creating scaled-down natural gas vehicles. It would become a proving ground for hydrogen and other renewable fuel sources and represents a community-based path to developing the infrastructure for these new fuels.

In the meantime, the rest of the world is using these vehicles and getting way ahead of the U.S. as a result.

This issue points to a need to look at all government regulations to see what can be done to get government out of the way of any such progress. The regulations developed over the last half a century have all served one purpose or another and many have unintended consequences. Some of these unintended consequences are keeping our country from creating solutions to the new challenges we are confronting. This is not to advocate for throwing the baby out with the bath water but for responsible leadership that maintains the right protections while resolving the unintended consequences that are counterproductive.

The times they are a changing, and it will take a concerted effort on all fronts to meet the challenges involved with adjusting to the new conditions.

Better Vehicles Coming?

One thing that slows people down about buying anything with new technology is that the next ones may be better products. This happened for the first two or three years of personal computers and with many other innovations. There are several things that come up about that.

One thing is that we are already three years into the third or fourth generation of electric vehicles. The first generation started in 1896 with the development of the first vehicle produced by Professor Ferdinand Porsche (yes THE Porsche), which was an electric vehicle. His second one was a serial hybrid!

The second thing is that the fuel savings start now, which means money ahead NOW. Similarly the tax savings happen right away, so that is money ahead now as well. You may be able to benefit from those now *but what about two years from now?*

Rick Sikes is a friend who asked me if I was upset that the price of the Volt was dropping. I laughed and offered the response that I have already saved that much in fuel and taxes, so what is the big deal.

Besides, I reminded him that I get to be one of the people who bought the first model. He was still working on getting his high-priced conversion to the everyday driving condition he wanted. Then again, Rick is the Fleet Superintendent for the City of Santa Monica, which is arguably one of the cleanest fleets on the planet. Rick is also one of the pillars of the EV advocacy world in Southern California and is setting the pace for the rest of the area.

The last consideration is that the tax credits may go away at any point or get reduced. It would not be the first thing killed due to budget issues and political changes.

At this point you have the information you need...
At this point you have the information you need to know whether you are interested in the EV solution. The next step would be to

look at what it takes to actually get one working in your life. There are two parts to this. One is the way that a particular EV would fit your transportation needs. The other is the nuts and bolts of actually using the vehicle. Both of these are covered in the next book in this series *Energy and EV Savings*. The best place to find that would be at www.energyandEVsecrets.com.

Links on EV Specs

Mileage Rating and Battery Testing Links
www.fueleconomy.gov/feg/evnews.shtml
www.standards.sae.org/j1634_201210?PC=VIDEO
www.Edmunds.com
www.epa.gov/nvfel/testing/dynamometer.htm
www1.eere.energy.gov/vehiclesandfuels/avta/light_duty/fsev/fsev_tests.html

US Department of Energy Idaho National Laboratory
Report on EV Range Changing factors
www.avt.inl.gov/pdf/fsev/auxiliary.pdf
www.avt.inl.gov/phev.shtml
www.avt.inl.gov/fsev.shtml

http://en.wikipedia.org/wiki/Ferdinand_Porsche

Additional Info

The Sustainable Transport Club

The Sustainable Transport Club is a network of people concerned about the issues presented in this book Energy and EV Secrets. The Club is working to create solutions to our dependence on oil. The network has helped to both create the information in this book and get this title into people's lives.

The Club is dedicated to creating a sustainable transportation system by way of outreach and education, community organizing, and helping our members to use sustainable transport in their daily lives.

We know that the pieces of such a system include bicycles, electric vehicles powered by solar, bio mass fuels, rail-based mass transit, converting green waste into energy, and breaking the grip that the automobile has on our culture.

The Sustainable Transport Club is bringing people and groups together to do this work through grassroots community action. The work is ongoing on several levels. It includes getting people to use the alternatives to oil, developing the technology, and establishing the businesses that support the sustainable solutions. It also involves helping the government facilitate the effort through the many roles that they play.

If you think we have this handled because we have a few Electric Vehicles (EVs) in the fleet, then please consider that EVs are being sold in the tens of thousands. The annual sale of gas vehicles is over 10 million and there are 255 million gas and diesel vehicles on the road in the U.S. alone.

We are far from done with our work.

The Club works when our people do what they can, when they can, to help create a sustainable future

Sign up now to become a bigger part of the solution by going to the website, www.sustainableclub.org and clicking on the Contact Us link.

General Links

Magazines and Other Info Sources
All Cars Electric   www.allcarselectric.com
Charged Electric Vehicles Magazine   www.chargedevs.com
Electric Cars Report   http://electriccarsreport.com
Electric Drive Transportation Association www.electricdrive.org
Electric Vehicle Blog
http://electric-vehicles-cars-bikes.blogspot.com
Electric Vehicles News www.electricvehiclesnews.com
ElectriClub News   http://electriclub.com/news/
Electrifying Times   www.electrifyingtimes.com
EV Album   www.evalbum.com
EV Charger News   www.evchargernews.com
EV Finder   www.evfinder.com
EV World   www.evworld.com/index.cfm
EV.com   www.ev.com
EV-motoring   http://ev-motoring.com
EVTV on YouTube   www.youtube.com/user/marionRickard
NY Times EV News
http://topics.nytimes.com/top/reference/timestopics/subjects/e/el
ectric_vehicles/index.html
Smart Grid News   www.smartgridnews.com
The Charging Point   www.thechargingpoint.com
The Three Laws of Batteries
http://gigaom.com/cleantech/the-three-laws-of-batteries-and-a-bonus-zero
th-law/
Topix Electric Car News   www.topix.com/autos/electric

Movies:
Revenge of the Electric Car www.revengeoftheelectriccar.com
Who Killed the Electric Car www.whokilledtheelectriccar.com
What is the Electric Car   www.whatistheelectriccar.com
Automotive X Prize   www.progressiveautoxprize.org

EV Video Link
www.youtube.com/user/KellyROlsen?feature=watch
Video on getting back outsourced jobs
https://youtube.googleapis.com/v/4FrGxO2Fn_M

Groups:
Electric Auto Association   www.electricauto.org
Electric Drive Transportation Association
                             www.electricdrive.org
Plug in America   www.pluginamerica.org
www.pluginamerica.org/why-plug-vehicles/ev-links-resources
Sustainable Transport Club   www.sustainableclub.org

Alphabet Soup
Acronyms and Technical Terms

There is a good bit of alphabet soup (meaning acronyms and technical specs) that go along with all of this. This is a bit dull by nature, so let's get that sorted out.

Vehicle Acronyms

AEV - All Electric Vehicle - New designation for full speed electric vehicle

BEV - Battery Electric Vehicle - Old designation for full speed electric vehicle

CEV - Conversion to Electric Vehicle - A gasoline powered vehicle that has been converted to electric drive

E-bike - Electric 2 wheel Vehicles - Includes electric versions of bicycles, mopeds, motorcycles and motor scooters

EV - Electric Vehicle - Any vehicle capable of being propelled by an electric drive motor

LSV - Low Speed Vehicle - Vehicles with 25 mph legal limit like a NEV, may include non-electric vehicles

MSEV - Medium Speed Electric Vehicle - Electric versions of MSVs that are faster than a NEV with substantially advance safety features

MSV - Medium Speed Vehicle - A proposed classification for MSV capable of 35 mph, possibly faster

NEV - Neighborhood Electric Vehicle - An all-electric LSV limited to street up to 35 mph

PHEV - Plug-in Hybrid Electric Vehicle - Vehicles with plug-in battery charging and an on-board generator

Basic Electricity

AC electricity - This is the kind of electricity used in homes and businesses. It is what gives power to most battery chargers.

DC electricity - This is the kind of electricity that batteries store and provide for an EV. DC electricity is more dangerous than the AC variety. (If you get shocked with AC you can let go of the wires more easily among other things.) The battery charger converts AC volts into DC volts, as part of the charging process.

Amps - This is an abbreviation of the word *amperes*. It describes the capacity that is available for moving electricity from one place to another. The higher the amp rating is, the more electricity that can be carried.

Volts -   The force behind the electricity. Science calls this the *electrical potential,* but if you ever get a high voltage shock you will know that force is involved. The more volts on a wire, the more electricity it can carry. The more volts, the more dangerous the electricity if it gets out of the wire.

Watts -   This is a unit of power that describes how much work can be done by the electricity. It can best be thought of as an amount of electricity. The amount of electricity available is equal to the force behind the supply multiplied times the capacity to move electricity from the supply to the place it is being used. This is expressed as Volts times Amps equals Watts.

kW -   This is an abbreviation for kilowatts. A kilowatt is a measure of power and it represents 1,000 watts. This is used to describe how much electricity a charger can provide or that a motor can use. Providing a 3.3 kW rate of charge for one hour puts 3.3 kWh into a battery.

kWh -   This is an abbreviation for kilowatt hour. It is a measure of how much electricity is provided or available at a given quantity for an hour. Battery packs are rated in kWh as that describes how much power can be supplied to the motor over time. That in turn determines how far the EV can travel. It is similar to how many gallons of gas in a gas tank. AEV 80s have battery packs capable of storing around 25 kWh.

Volts, Amps and Watts are named after an Italian, a French man and a Scots man. So what do you get when they all walk into a room? Probably a big charge!

Battery Pack Related

DOD -   This stands for Depth of Discharge. A fifty percent Depth of Discharge means you have used half your battery capacity. An eighty percent depth of discharge means you only have twenty percent of the battery charge left in the system.

SOC -   This stands for State of Charge. A one hundred percent state of charge (100% SOC) means the battery is totally full; ten percent state of charge means you better be real close to a charger.

SOC meter -   This is a display that shows how much charge you have left. It might use percentages or it might use lights for this purpose. Some will use numbers as well. A State of Charge (SOC) meter will normally display the amount of charge that can actually be used by your vehicle. There may be more electricity in the battery for emergency and other reasons.

Here is a look at the current list of books planned for this series:

Book One: **Energy and EV Secrets, How the Volt, plug-in Hybrids, electric cars and e-bikes can save energy and cut your gas prices.**

Part I, *Energy Secrets*
This section shows why Energy will be a defining concern for the next decades. It brings the issue home to jobs, the economy and our personal bank accounts.

Part II, *EV Secrets*
This is focused on a solution to our current dependence on oil. The EV (Electric Vehicle) Solution will work for millions of people in their personal lives. When millions of people solve this for themselves, then we are creating a solution at the level of the national economy.

Book Two: **Energy and EV Savings**
(Due in 2014)
How to Beat High Gas Prices with an Electric Vehicle
It gets down to YOUR facts and figures so you will know just how and when an EV fits your needs. The book would let people work through the wires and plugs as well as the Kilowatts and MPGe to see exactly how an EV would fit in their lives. It will also explore the EV to solar PV connection to show how quickly you can get to free fuel by driving on sunshine.

Book Three: **EVs and the Environment**
(Coming Soon!)
The third book will lay out how the EV Solution fits in with environmental issues. It should be released soon after *Book Two*.

About the Author

Russell Sydney is uniquely qualified to write about the burgeoning Electric Vehicle (EV) Solution.

Russell is a seasoned and experienced writer and international seminar leader. He has a gift for turning technical information into readily usable and understandable language. He has been the Editor and Principle Writer for the Sustainable Transport Club Newsletter since 2004. He is the author of the best-selling Bust the Y2K Bug and A History of the Farmers Markets Movement in California.

His professional career has included rising to the top of the training field. Russell has trained people on technology throughout the United States, all across Canada, around the U.K., and down into the Caribbean. This work helped over 300 companies adopt new technologies and over 8,000 people with various aspects of business and computerization.

Russell Sydney also helped create one of the leading Electric Vehicle Areas in the U.S. This EV Area stretches from Long Beach to Santa Monica and up to Santa Barbara. He has worked with many of the top EV leaders and developers as well as hundreds of EV drivers around the country. He is communicating their knowledge, in addition to his own personal experience. He is a Chevy Volt driver and has been driving and testing all sorts of EVs since 2003.

Russell Sydney has a Master's Degree in International Development from UC Davis.